BULLOCK CARTS TO BOEINGS
- An Octogenarian's Journey

Nirmala Ramaswamy

INDIA • SINGAPORE • MALAYSIA

ISBN 979-8-89067-887-4

All credits for the cover pages of the book and the Images are as follow:

1. Cover Generated using AI
2. Images – Black panther, Monitor Lizard, Festival of colours – Holi, Women Scientist at work – Shutter Stock.com

Dedication

I dedicate this book to my loving parents, my father. G. Gopalaswami who not only inculcated the habit of reading in me, but also encouraged me to pursue my love for creative arts, crafts and creative writing too. My mother Krishnamma was a role model mother so very dedicated to the family. They both bestowed all their affection and attention on our upbringing. I feel indebted to them forever.

Contents

Preface

I was born when our country was a colony of the British empire, but grew up in a free and democratic India. I might have listened to the famous speech of our first prime minister Jawaharlal Nehru given on 14th Aug '47 on the eve of India's independence about India's tryst with destiny. "At the stroke of the midnight hour..........India will awaken to life and freedom", but there I was alive but not awake, not even aware of neither freedom nor bondage as I was a little girl.

Well, this book is the story of the experiences I have been through in my long life as a child, a student, a young girl, bride and as a homemaker, the rest of my life.

I heard from my father the story of how India, which was one of the most ancient yet highly advanced countries a couple of thousand years back, was the richest nation in the world. It was religious and traditional yet did not isolate herself. Its prosperity and riches attracted invaders who marched in through the Khyber pass in the Himalayas. Traders took the sea route from all directions and carried on trade for thousands of years. Pilgrims used all possible approaches from West, East, North and South. Scholars and eager students poured in from all around to study in our oldest universities, Nalanda and Taxila.

Ultimately a stage came when our country was impoverished and reduced to the state of struggling to gain freedom from the colonial rulers. The readers know how the father of the nation lead the people in a non -violent war and won freedom from British rule.

Once the country became free it started its slow march towards progress and after more than seven decades has come to be recognised as a nation developing fast and hoping to lead the world in the 21st century. I have tried to express in this memoirs of mine, how the landmark changes influenced and improved the lifestyles of its citizens.

I would say my mother's and grandmothers' generations had a lot of hardships to face. They had to clean, wash and cook a lot of complicated recipes in those age old heavy brass and bronze utensils, cast iron pans and stone and mud pots. They had to pound and powder grains using pestles and other heavy iron tools. They used iron implements to do their chores around the kitchen. They were perhaps remnants from Stone Age, Iron Age and Bronze Age, ideally and conveniently shaped and sturdy but too heavy and cumbersome to handle. Cooking with firewood and charcoal as fuel sitting on the floor in smoky kitchens was no joke. They did not have any of the electric and electronic home appliances that are available to us now to do the million chores in and around the kitchen and the house in general. But I must say, they mostly remained physically fit till 60 or 70 at least.

Our generation was lucky indeed. As I have already mentioned, we started our married lives with stainless steel utensils, gas stoves, mixies, toasters and hot plates etc. The age of electronics followed. Transistors and record players were introduced. Then came the three-in-ones, VCR's, DVD's, stereophonic music systems etc., not that we could buy them immediately, but some years later at least they entered our living rooms. We were absolutely thrilled when we bought a black and white TV set in the early 80's.

We were awestruck when we saw the bulky desktop computer in the 90's, to be followed by their progeny, consisting of laptop, Chromebook, iPad, kindle and smartphones in the new millennium. In short, televisions, computers and stereophonic music systems for entertainment, cell phones and 'WhatsApp' for fast communication and jet planes for faster transportation etc., came into use mostly in the last 20 to 30 years, mostly in the 21st century.

I have seen and. been through the gradual change in the progress. In my childhood, I mean in the earlier years after independence I literally ran to take or make a call from the telephone which had a bulky bakelite base with a rotary dial. Even in the 60's and 70's such bakelite phones were there. Missed calls used to remain mysterious calls. If I missed a call, I used to make 10 calls to find out who called. Hey, how slim, sleek, light and colourful today's smartphone looks, carrying a load of information except perhaps the horoscope of the person calling, on its face. Today in our country millions possess mobile phones and millions have gas connections. Millions have television sets. Radio was our only source of entertainment in our childhood. Some of today's children have theatres at home.

Though we did not have toys, dolls, video games, we had a lot of human interaction with siblings, cousins and friends. We played in the open in the lap of nature. We were free birds. We did not spend the whole evening attending Maths or Physics classes or coaching classes for music, cricket, tennis or swimming. We were not constantly told to excel and achieve. There was nobody to dictate all the time what I should do with my free time. We were not pressurised and stressed out.

This does not mean India did not have the facilities. Indian schools, colleges and other training institutions have always had a very high standard. India tried to keep up with the advanced countries in developments, but with a multimillion population, poverty, illiteracy and scarcity of food, clothing and shelter for millions of people, the pace of progress was rather slow initially. I would go further to say there was a lack of unity among people, a slight lack of civic sense and awareness. Many times, those in power who had perhaps the authority to take action or administer were not accessible and easily available to listen to the grievances of the common man.

Natural disasters like storms, cyclones and cloudbursts can be sudden and unexpected but the cities and towns do not seem to be prepared for even the much expected monsoon. When the roads are flooded and the houses are inundated it is the common man and the poorer people who face the brunt of the calamity in full force. If the authorities in charge take care of repairing the roads, clearing the storm grains, removing non-biodegradable trash and keep an eye on the level of water flowing in the rivers and stored in the reservoirs on a 'regular basis', it would help the citizens and their properties to remain safe. Nobody can keep replenishing their belongings in the form of their basic necessities like household utensils, clothes, gadgets and vehicles like two wheelers or cars etc. again and again.

On the other hand when every effort is being made by the people in power to provide roads, toilets, water supply and electricity to the people living even in remote corners of this vast country, the public who use them have to cooperate in conserving, maintaining and preserving all these properly.

The law that children from the age of 6 to 14 should be given free education was a great move. Providing a free meal in the school was a greater idea. The best move was to make people send their daughters to school. Slogans like 'Beti bachao', beti padao' made us heave a sigh of relief. Only if women get enlightened and empowered, the families can be motivated and the country can move forward.

Scientists and researchers have done wonders to make us proud and keep our heads high like the citizens of the most advanced nations of the world. Chandrayaan did what it was told to do. Aditya is heading straight in its designated path to do what it is meant and sent to do. Indian women have done extremely well in every field from sports arena to space arena. The Indian vaccine named Covaccin saved not only our people from the attack of Covid -19 but millions around the world from being hit by the deadly virus.

But we cannot do away with the institutions which have been built over thousands of years based on our fundamental faith, beliefs, trust, hopes and aesthetic sense to lead our lives in a meaningful manner laying emphasis on the spiritual side of humanity too.

Now the stage has come where we have to think and constantly remember what is good for the health and survival of our planet. Now we seniors are fortunate to be living in 21st century. We must remember that our millennial grandchildren, born in this 21st century are growing up looking forward to a glorious, prosperous, happy, healthy and peaceful future. They should live better than us. It becomes our aim and responsibility to preserve our planet green and clean for th e future generations. We have to work collectively and consciously to preserve the earth and hand it over to posterity in great shape, so that they continue to live happily on this wonderful planet.

Acknowledgements

My husband always encouraged me to hone my talents and let me hold exhibitions of arts, crafts and flower arrangements in various cities of our country. I must acknowledge the great help and support he rendered morally, technologically and of course financially in this venture of publishing my two books. This second book I would not have been able to do without his computer support through and through.

My brother Dr. Lakshmipathi, a well known humorist has been responsible for constantly reminding us about the humour aspect in human lives. If there is anything in a lighter vein, be sure growing up with him and my other brothers and sister has not gone in vain. We laughed a lot together. My brother Ram Mohan insisted that I should go ahead and publish this book, no matter how good or bad it is. Maybe he wasn't sure which category it would belong to.

I troubled my sons Shankar and Arvind to read my narrative and give their feedback and opinions. I asked my daughters-in-law, Meena and Sirisha to read my write up and give their valuable suggestions. I have had interesting comments and a number of suggestions from my entire family, each one pulling me in a different direction. My sons helped me decide the title and even design the cover of this book.

I have to thank my grandchildren for being my inspiration. Actually they are the main reason for which I started the whole project. My granddaughters Aditi, Shreya, Priyanka and my grandson Ananth kept insisting the narration should be humorous. Whenever I felt like giving it up as it was not turning out to be humorous, it was Aditi who motivated me to finish and publish at all costs.

My niece Krishna Desiraju went through the narrative patiently in the midst of her own busy schedules of assisting her husband publish his books. She gave me solid support by giving her positive comments and constructive criticism. My niece Indu Gargeya kept calling me from across the Atlantic and persuaded me to go on with my idea of describing my life experiences in the form of a book. My nieces Sundari and Sita gave their ideas and helped me with photographs. My cousins Lalitha, Aruna, Prakash and Sundar gave me some very precious pictures from the past. I must thank Swarna and Gauri for giving colourful photos of our festivals and of the Mehndi ceremony observed before wedding celebrations these days.

Shashikala, Chandra and Geetha, my childhood friends, supplied such colourful photographs of whatever I required with great enthusiasm including one of our old Herald car. I must acknowledge the great help rendered to me by my friends Shantha Jayaram and Hamsalatha Krishnan. Shantha gave me many relevant pictures of village homes, huge utensils and other village scenes. Hamsa composed them into collages. I thank all of you from the bottom of my heart for your kind and encouraging help in my endeavour. Readers, the subject I have taken up is too vast and I, as an octogenarian home maker, I could only touch the tip of the iceberg.

I have a circle of close friends from childhood who have been a part of my life all through. Maybe we had a lot of influence rubbing off on each other. I must acknowledge the role of the teachers in our school who tried to shape us to be wholesome personalities. I have learnt a lot from my friends in the Air Force about teamwork, good grooming, doing up the interiors and cooking. I could pick up a little of their culture like their languages, folk music and folk dance.

In fact the millions I have come across in all crowded places have given me enough food for thought.

This country with all its diversity, beauty, divinity and traditionality has made me what I am.

I pray that any number of births I take should be on this 'punya bhoomi' with the same loving family around me. The Kapali temple close to which I lived and I studied has unknowingly embraced me in its fold forever.

01

Dawn of My Life......

The Magnificent Dawn

The memories of my long life are like scattered pieces of a colourful jigsaw puzzle of sights and sounds. I see them very clearly in my dreams sometimes, but at other times they are foggy. Now after ages, I decided to recapture the various moods, dimensions and flavours of my experiences in words.

I shall begin my narration from the dawn of my life; almost around the time our nation broke free from the British Empire to become a democratic republic. I hope this story will capture the imaginations of children born in the 21st century. They are two or three generations moved from mine growing up in an entirely different atmosphere. In fact, they were not only born in a different millennium, but also into a fast-changing world.

As a child I lived with my parents on a street about a kilometre away from the ancient Kapaleeswara Temple in Mylapore, a well-known suburb of what was then called Madras. This temple and those located in Thiruvallikeni, Thiruvanmiyur, George Town and scores of others are said to be more than 1500 years old. These suburbs might have grown around these ancient sites of worship. Long ago, before this growth happened in pockets, Madras itself was nothing more than a small fishing village along the coast of Bay of Bengal. The village was named after a fisherman by the name of "Madrasan", and it was originally known as "Madrasapatanam". Subsequently the name was shortened to Madras. Although the name was changed to Chennai, for an old timer like me, it will forever remain Madras.

The city was part of the region of "Tondaimandalam", ruled first by the Pallavas and then the seafaring Cholas. By the time the British first set foot in the area, the Nayak chieftains of Vijayanagar Empire had taken over the entire area.

The British arrived with the intent of setting up a warehouse and starting strong trade links with our country. That's what they are supposed to have told the local population then. They found a plot of land, ideally situated along the sea shore to develop into a township, and bought it from a Nayak chieftain called "Damarla Venkatadri Nayaka", son of "Chennappa Nayaka".

The port of Madras was hardly a stone's throw from this area, and they could land their ships beautifully and start their trading company. But it was not a warehouse they built: they constructed a towering fortress which laid the foundation for building their future empire on Indian soil. They established the "East India Company in India". The town inside the citadel was known as the 'White town'. Outside the walls it was the 'Black town'. Ultimately Fort St. George, which the British began building in 1639–40 CE, turned out to be the beginning of British colonisation of India.

Now I will leap forward in time by more than 300 years, to my story. Mylapore was an ancient, quiet, friendly and beautiful suburb of Madras. Our house was the first one on a street called "Vedanta Desikar Street", more popularly known as "Pelathope". It was just wide enough to let two small cars scrape through side by side. There were street houses on both sides of the road with their gates opening right onto the street. Most of them shared a common wall between them. Generally such street houses surrounded the temples and temple tanks which belonged to the temples.

There were four main roads called 'Mada Veedis' around the temple. They were quite broad since they were used during the temple festivals for taking a procession of the 'utsava vigrahams' (bronze idols) in chariots and palanquins. The main roads and the parallel bylanes peeling off from them joined yet another main road at the other end. This formed some sort of grid. 'Pelathope' was a blind by lane close to North (Vadakku) 'Mada Street, (Veedi)'.

Our two-storey house had an open terrace on the third floor where we used to sleep during the sweltering heat of peak summer. On our terrace stood an enclosure with short walls built with bricks. The upper half of the short walls was closed with bamboo mats, topped with a thatched roof. With a gentle sea breeze blowing across, in summer, it used to be a very cool place to sleep in our house. It served as my eldest brother's study room as well. The view from the parapet wall on the east side was quite panoramic, as we could see the majestic "Kapali" temple 'Gopuram' raising above all the houses on North Mada street. The stunning view from our terrace is one piece of the jigsaw puzzle that remains bright and clear in my brain.

Pelathope, meaning 'jackfruit garden', might have been a garden of jackfruit trees earlier, but we did not see any such tree. All we could see were quaint houses, each with a wooden or metal gate which opened into a little cemented open space. A raised platform with pillars was there after this. This was the 'verandah', after which stood the heavy wooden door. There was a bright white 'kolam' (rangoli) at the entrance to every house. A couple of bungalows at the end of the road were quite huge with open space and garden all around. There was the temple of 'Vedanta Desikar' facing the street right at the top end. The temple door was opened for public only once a year for a special 'Darshanam' followed by a procession of the idol down the street. We used to look forward to this ceremonial opening.

We were a very close knit family living in the house interacting a lot. I lived with my parents, four elder brothers, and an elder sister. I was the youngest child. My mother's elder sister lived with us, as she had lost her husband when she was in her thirties. She had no children of her own, and became an inseparable member of our family from then on. A few years later when my paternal grandpa passed away, my grandma joined us. Our house was crowded with family members, every room brimming with the lively chattering of grandparents, aunts, and children alike. My brothers were always talking, walking or chatting with my mother in the dining room or conducting raucous arguments among them about which team would win the test match at 'Chepauk' or who was a better batsman etc.

Life was quite simple in every household, with menfolk, I mean the patriarch, reading the newspaper early in the morning, sipping hot coffee from a brass or silver glass. As part of the morning ritual, the doting wife would bring out a 'dabara', in which the glass of coffee stood, and set them on a small table, called' a 'teapoy', in front of the husband. My father was very particular about the brand of coffee powder used and how thick the decoction should be. Like King Arthur and the Holy Grail, he was constantly on the lookout for the mythical 'perfect' blend. It almost became a ceremony in our household.

The minute my dad took the first sip he would say,

"Emey", why is the coffee not so good today?". As a small girl, I used to find it funny and wonder what could possibly go so drastically wrong with a simple mix of coffee powder and milk. One day it would be that the milk was more than the decoction. The next day his complaint would be that it was too strong and bitter, with too much decoction and not enough sugar. I feel in general men fuss about a perfect 'cuppa' a lot. Till today, the lord of my house asks me every day why the coffee is "not so good today?" Same words and they do ring a bell!!!

Those days milk was fresh in all homes, coming straight from a cow's udders to us. There were no bottles or cartons of milk available in milk booths or grocery stores. If it was diluted with water by the milkman it was sold as 'kaippaal', or "hand-milk", and it was sold at a cheaper rate than the undiluted stuff. My mother never bought 'kaipaal', opting instead for the freshest and thickest milk available.

Our milkman would bring a cow or (later) a buffalo to our doorstep before sunrise, milk it, and give it to us. His name was 'Venu', and despite his protests, my mother knew, like any other milkman, he kept water at the bottom of his milking can. How Venu could swirl his can with a skilful sleight of hand before milking to show it was absolutely empty not spilling one spoon of the water, remained a mystery for my mother, aunt or anyone who had to stand near the gate before he started milking the cow. My mother said that the semi-darkness at dawn, and her-sleepy state at that hour, must have helped him a lot in his milky machinations. She would not pick up a fight with him though, so he continued to be our milkman for ages. She thought perhaps at least Venu used clean water, others may not.

My mother had to bustle around and get us ready to go to school or college. My eldest brother entered college when I was in class 1. We took our hot coffee, cocoa, 'Horlicks' or 'Ovaltine', in short, whatever beverage 'Amma' gave us. She always knew what each one's preferences were. We did not have a dinner table back then to clutter up with plates, glasses and cups with leftover liquids and solids. We had to leave all our dirty dishes in the wash area. In some households-thankfully not ours - the children were supposed to wash them before leaving them there. Once the table came to the dining room, we had one more surface to be cluttered, and our eating style itself changed. We just left everything carelessly on the table, to be picked up and washed later by whoever could not tolerate the clutter.

In our dining-table-less era we had to be served a solid brunch anytime between 8 to 9 am. One by one we would appear at the kitchen door to remind my mother. The food would be served on our plates and we were seated on the floor. Our lunch boxes had to be packed and kept ready for school. It must have been quite a task for every mother, as the number of kids in each household those days was anywhere between five to ten, or even twelve. In any case, the mornings were hectic for the whole family.

With only two school going children, I found my mornings hectic when they were small. I cannot even imagine the stress of those mothers of the past dealing with six to twelve hungry mouths!!!

The day dawned for our parents before sunrise, whether it was winter or summer. In the early morning I used to see men carrying cloth and gunny bags to go to fetch veggies fresh from the main market. They went that early to cut costs, as the door delivery was far more expensive and offered less choice in produce. Out of convenience, though, my mother chose to buy from the hawkers who came to our doorstep. These vegetable sellers and street vendors would start their business by 6.30 am., if not earlier. Unlike in most other businesses back then, men and women were equal in this enterprise. In fact, we had more women than men selling vegetables in cities like Madras.

There was a lot of interaction between the seller and buyer at that time, with loud haggling occurring on each household's doorstep early in the morning. Since the sellers were often regulars who showed up every day for years on end, the customers grew familiar with them and felt comfortable bargaining to pick the best beans and brinjals for the lowest possible prices. Ours was the first house on their route, so perhaps my mother got the freshest beans of them all. In fact, except for groceries from the neighbourhood shops, we did not have to walk or drive long distances for our daily needs, including snacks and toiletries. Essential, though fancy, items like combs, needles, mirrors, safety pins, press buttons and 'bindis' were also sold by street hawkers at the doorstep.

My brothers walked to the boys' school and my elder sister walked with me to the girl's school in the first year or two of my schooling. She finished her schooling after that. Both boys' and girls' schools were in the neighbourhood. We did not have to worry about heavy traffic on the roads or getting run over by zooming cars. We had a shoulder bag, not a backpack with a ton of books bending our backs. Menfolk walked across to take the bus to the office and women and children used the hand pulled rickshaw for going anywhere close by, especially to places like the family doctor's clinic early in the morning. The roads had some bus traffic and there were very few cars floating by. We came across posh looking Pontiac, Dodge, Chevrolet, Plymouth and Ford Austin cars on the roads in the pre-independence era and for years later. Our own Premier 'Padmini', Fiat, Standard Herald and the most popular Ambassadors were yet to appear. They arrived perhaps ten to fifteen years later.

I cannot recollect much from my early childhood except very hazy scenes like these from here and there. I might have gathered lots of information about the past from our collection of photographs or my elder siblings talking about it during mealtimes. It was an all-time favourite subject for us.

But one scene which is vivid in my mind from the early days of the post-Independence era is Mahatma Gandhi's sudden and tragic end on 30th Jan.'48. Everyone in our family was moved to tears after listening to the radio announcement of the assassination that evening. The news shocked all of us beyond belief and evoked a lot of emotional outbursts and tears. It was spoken about for a long time in our house and neighbourhood. Maybe it left a deep impact on my impressionable mind as it was almost a similar situation I remembered which happened even earlier. It is a very hazy scene of my mother weeping aloud when she came to know her father passed away. It scared me a lot.

In our home we children were asked to assemble in our 'Pooja' room and sing 'Raghupathi Raghava Rajaram,' every Friday evening at 6 o' clock for several months after the tragic event of Gandhi's sudden death. In our school we were taught to spin yarn from a length of compressed cotton with the help of a handheld gadget called 'takli'. Perhaps it was a homage we paid to Mahatma Gandhi on his death anniversary the following year. We could not spin much. It called for a lot of skill.

My paternal grandpa died a year after the father of the nation. I could not understand how all of sudden my loving grandpa could disappear forever. When my father wept I got so worried and scared. I was packed off to my aunt's place. I missed him too much and death was still a sort of mystery to me.

The father of the nation

02

Childhood and Schooling

Childhood is as much about school as it is about home. When I completed 5 years, I was promptly admitted to class 1 in a very popular girls' school, the school my elder sister went to. Before that I vaguely remember going to a Montessori school for a few months but I don't know why I did not go for the whole year. Actually I don't remember much about this school except the teacher's face and a name,. I associate with her. We could wear a full length skirt or a frock in the elementary school I went to. I walked the same route for all 11 years of my schooling. I could have walked blindfolded too. It was quite possible as the school was in the same spot and we stayed put in the same house for more than 23 years or so, though our family was expanding. Our school building became bigger too with many additional structures as it was a very popular school in the neighbourhood. My brothers did the same; I mean they went to the most famous boys' schools nearby. But their elementary school was different from the high school they went to.

I remember day 1 in Class 1 in my school. Sniffling and wiping my cheeks every minute with the back of my hand, I quietly held on to my sister's hand tightly, not letting her go to her class in high school. Somehow she found another little girl and told her to be my friend and that girl called 'Gayatri' took my hand in hers as though she was taking charge and took me inside the classroom and sat next to me. We had to sit on the floor but each one of us had a desk in front. She was my only friend on day 1 and she remained one of my good friends in school. Soon I made more friends of course and I settled down happily.

We had no separate playground but we had a huge shady area close to our airy and open class rooms without doors. Under the trees we had a seesaw, a ladder, a slide and a swing. Climbing trees and plucking the fruits and pods was what the boys loved to do. We had them, I mean the boys and the trees, one fig tree and one huge tamarind tree and a huge 'toongumoonji maram' which when translated into English would be 'sleepy-faced tree'. Up to class 3 we had coeducation in our school. We had to wait for our turn to sit on the swing and we girls would swing gently. Some naughty girl or boy would push it with force from behind all of a sudden. The screams and giggles of children remain as sound bytes in my brain. Kick starting the seesaw or ladder to tease the opponent with a jerky movement was another favourite joke of many naughty children. It was fun though.

Of course we had a lot of learning to do in school. We all started 'at the very beginning, a very good place to start' as a popular song goes and we began with our alphabets in Tamil to be followed by ABC in English, a couple of years later. We used to write with a 'balapam' (a breakable slate pencil) on the slate which could be wiped any number of times with our palms and fingers. We were not given notebooks and pencils but only slates and soft slate pencils for class work. But for homework, whatever little we had, we used notebooks and pencils. Perhaps, they believed small children need not waste money on notebooks and pencils and waste wood for making paper and pencils too. Mind you we had huge trees in our school premises and we loved them.

What I mean is in our generation we were in airy classrooms and played under trees. The way we see trees being felled today makes us sad really. Wasting paper is also a bad habit.

We had to get our multiplication tables by heart. That was tough indeed as we had to memorise from 1 to 12 tables to start with and then we went up to 16 tables and then tables for fractions. This last one was the toughest. We did not have a calculator ever. There was nothing to aid us with our math problems except our parents and teachers' scolding. My children learnt their tables by heart too.

And throughout our school life we carried our lunch box. In our part of the country, it was mixed rice, rice and Sambar or rice and curds called 'Thayir sadam' that we girls and boys took day after day. The day we took idlis, dosas, 'chapattis' or Uthappam, we had to exchange with a close group of friends as we all sat together on the floor in a corridor. Pickles and papads were picked from each other's boxes freely.

The minute I reached home in the evening I threw the canvas shoulder bag, and enjoyed 'puries', 'pakoras', or 'upuma' waiting for me. I gulped them down and ran out to hop and skip again with my neighbourhood friends till darkness set in. But, well, that was when I was in elementary classes.

But I had to grow up and of course I did learn to be more mature. Slowly I understood the jokes my brothers cracked and the topics which my father took up to discuss while eating. When I was nine or ten I started really enjoying dinner time. It was a really fun time for us. We laughed a lot and six of us sitting on the floor and having our dinner would not wash our hands till the rice and curd dried on our palms. We always had a conversation going on while eating. On Sundays and holidays we mostly had lunch together.

We sat on wooden planks called 'peeta' 'in Telugu, 'Manai' in Tamil. We tried to cling to one plate as 'my own plate' and ate from that only day after day. Lots of arguments and fights for favourite spots took place but it was only till our father joined us taking his seat in his reserved spot like we have a spot for the head of the family at the head of the table now. It was some discipline which every family followed.

I recollect how my patriotic father, a lawyer by profession, used to talk a lot about the country, its progress, general elections, political parties, leaders, ideologies and problems like corruption the nation was facing etc. The corruption issue troubled him a lot. He instilled in all of us a love for the motherland by his emotional and inspiring talks during our meal times on holidays. He made us feel by his own behaviour that we had to be sincere, honest and morally upright. Another fact my parents strongly believed was that it was essential to be loving and nurture relationships and friendships.

Freedom of our country meant a fresh beginning of life, full of hopes for a wonderful future, not only for the nation but for the young people of the country. Maybe that was the message my father wanted to convey. I could not fully appreciate and understand any of these earlier as a little girl but I listened to him spellbound. He was a good orator with a thundering voice, a lawyer that he was! His gestures are still fresh in my memory.

While in school, we were asked by my father to read a lot on our own. Always parents want children to read while the latter want to play outside or inside the homes. I told my children to read and later I saw them asking their children to read books. My father insisted we read books, newspapers and magazines in Tamil and English that were bought by him. The trouble was there was too much reading material back home. My father was a voracious reader and he wanted me to read 'War and peace', a voluminous book, which I could not lift and hold even. My brothers loved to buy comics which were from outside the country too. It was second hand I presume. Laurel and Hardy comics called 'Film Fun' were their favourite. They used to go to 'Moore market', a very exciting shopping centre in Madras selling interesting things including second hand books. My brothers used to watch lots of comedy films from Hollywood featuring Buster Keaton, Groucho Marx, Dean Martin and Jerry Lewis. My sister got married very young when I was a little girl. At home I spent more time with my brothers. I remember being grumpy about staying home when they went to a movie. They would say that I was too young to follow and understand the jokes. My father loved Charlie Chaplin movies and he has taken me to see them. I saw a lot of Tamil cinema comedians on the screen as I was taken to Tamil movies in a nearby theatre by my mother sometime but mostly with her brother and aunt. Any uncle and aunt who visited and stayed with us from out-station wanted to see movies in a nearby theatre. We had two of the theatres within walking distance.

Cracking jokes and narrating funny incidents of the day in his clinic by my eldest doctor brother was a regular feature at dinner time. I was in my early teens then. He had a clinic of his own those days and he described the idiosyncrasies and fears of the patients in a funny manner. The other three brothers came out with their own jokes in college and schools.

Ah, well that was the way we grew up laughing a lot.

It remains an unforgettable era indeed and we siblings keep talking about it a lot whenever we meet.

It was the dawn of my life in our loving home.

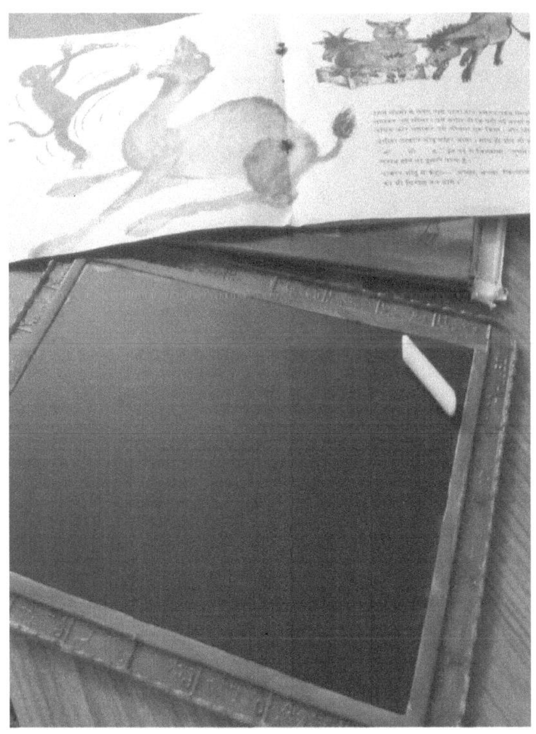

We used slates and 'Balpams' for class work in elementary classes

We loved to Laugh

03

Hurray, Hurray, Happy Holidays

Actually the summer vacation was such that everyone was stuck in the house due to the heat. Nobody dared to venture out. All schools and colleges were closed. The high court had a month-long vacation. Even my father who would be in his office room most of the mornings and evenings used to come down and take a break after his brunch and short nap.

He was a disciplinarian but he enjoyed the company of people including children. He never believed in wasting time and he had quite a few hobbies. That was the time when we kids, I mean a lot of boys and girls from down the street assembled in our house for indoor games. The evenings were for the boys to play cricket on the street. That was their passion. Perhaps each one of them thought he was going to hit the headlines in the sports page of the dailies the next day. Maybe with a little bit of luck, he may hit headlines in the front page, a 'debut century' or something dramatic like that. While in reality our 'Pelathope 11' could probably throw or hit the ball with all their might and they might have hurt the innocent pedestrians and got shouted at by them.

Friendly neighbours understood and compromised. When the ball fell inside one particular neighbour's compound, he didn't applaud this boy's huge sixer, but came out to shout at the boy. But it never became a major issue as there was no playground nearby, so he also understood. My brothers invented a game of cricket inside the house in which they bowled calling out names of the best bowlers and batsmen of the 40's like Lindwall, Valentine, Bradman or Mankad, Hazare and Amarnath. They played cricket sitting on the floor hitting the wall opposite with a ball. It used to amuse me.

But we had other indoor games for the hot daytime during 'Agni nakshatram', touching 40 to 45 degree C. The kids who were eager to play carom board had to compete with each other to prove their skill to be chosen as a partner by the champion among the group. Otherwise they had to play 'pallankuzhi', a clever game calling for a lot of calculations. Boys, including my brothers, played cards (a lot of cheating was involved) or Trade, called 'Monopoly' now. Aunts joined in for playing 'Noughts and Crosses' (tic-tac-toe) or 'Snakes and ladders' with other girls. Our desi version was called 'parama pada sobhana padam'. There were many interesting games which required just 7 big seeds and 'skilful' fingers. Another favourite game was 'dayakattai' (chaupar), a game of dice, played from the days of the legendary Mahabharata, for which we did not even require a board. It was drawn on the floor with a piece of chalk. Lots of laughter and jokes could be heard. The hall was throbbing with life. The decibel level must have been quite high. People generally tolerated high decibel levels in the neighbourhood in the past.

I presume staying for long periods in the same house and neighbourhood had its own advantages. Childhood friendships remained strong. In fact we are still in touch. This is my personal opinion. The hawkers and vendors of puffed rice, groundnuts, cotton candy, 'palm fruit' and ice fruit timed their visit beautifully starting from 11am to 4pm, when the heat was maximum. The ice fruit is our desi version of popsicles of today. When we sucked it, the juice will come out and the stick will be left with a blob of ice melting by the seconds. We would not have taken it then, perhaps, if we thought about the hygiene aspect of it. To be honest the exterior of the flask was not exactly clean.

Somehow that image remains in my brain. The palm fruit called ‘nungu’, the slippery jelly fruit, was a great treat we all loved. These ‘nungus’ could be washed under the running water but if we punctured them by mistake the juice would pour out from the tender ‘nungu’ and go down the drain with the water. I used to be in hurry to eat and poked the palm fruit many times and would regret a lot.

The sticky and gooey ‘cotton candy’ in shocking pink colour was made in front of our gate but the candy maker did use his bare fingers and a cloth during the process. There was a time when we had them every day but once four of us had typhoid fever starting on the same day; my doctor brother put a ban on cotton candy and ice fruit too.

One of my father’s hobbies was stamp collection. He never threw the postal envelopes which were delivered at our doorstep. But peeling the stamps from them and sticking them in an album was time consuming. While we played, my father would come down in the afternoons and play an indoor game like ‘pallanguzhi’ for a while. Then he would move on to the postal envelopes and the trays of water in the other half of the room. The boys would be curious and they would come and sit around. He would teach them how to cut the stamped edges from envelopes, soak them in water and peel them gently. He used to ask them to develop a healthy hobby and give them a few stamps to start their collection. They could have a chat with him.

One of my brothers who used to help our father from childhood in this venture became an avid collector of stamps. As he grew older his interest and collections also grew but he did not have the children in the neighbourhood soaking, peeling and drying the stamps for him. He had his 'better half 'of course by his side.

Years rolled by. My brothers joined professional degree courses in different colleges. I came to high school too. The carefree afternoons were rare to come by. From class 6 the number of subjects I had to study increased to six, out of which three were languages. The new entrant Sanskrit seemed to be simple as we could score 90% or more in the beginning. But as we progressed I found the grammar very tough. The ten tenses and moods, the eight cases for nouns called 'Sabdams' had to be learnt by heart. We had to do the 'vigraha vakyam.' which was splitting a compound word into its individual components. The derivation was clear but difficult because the word had to be divided in a meaningful way.

When we were in class 8, which was called 'III rd. form', we had to start learning Hindi also. It was made compulsory; though writing the final exam was optional. We girls used to get confused between Sanskrit and Hindi a lot. In high school we had a lot of extracurricular activities. So I never came home before five o'clock or later sometimes. Our annual day, sports day, competitions of sorts, making a hand-written class magazine, a science and art exhibition held annually, lectures and discourses by eminent personalities etc. kept us very busy. We had to keep the school corridors clean class rooms clean, fill up drinking water in the drums, check whether the quadrangle was clean. Well, we had a team of girls chosen to look after these activities. Such work taught us team work, responsibility, creativity, hygiene and discipline. Our teachers were so dedicated and took personal interest. We had an unforgettable time in school indeed!

When we passed our 11thClass which was called SSLC (Secondary School leaving Certificate) examination, we finished with our schooling and came out ready to join the pre-university course in a college to be followed by graduation.

When I think back, I realise how undisturbed my school years were for me and how different it was for my two sons. My husband perhaps changed his school once but I walked to the same school from the same house for 11 years, my children went to 6 different schools in 6 different states speaking six different languages. Thankfully learning the local language was not compulsory. The house they went from was anywhere between a room in the officers' mess to a three bedroom bungalow. The 'vahaan' they rode on was anything from a cycle rickshaw, taxi, a two wheeler, an Air Force bus to a 3 tonne truck. Only the school uniform remained the same throughout India for the students of Kendriya Vidyalaya.

While the elder son went to three different schools for his KG classes as the circumstances were such, the younger one had his entire schooling in Kendriya Vidyalaya from KG to XII. The convent and other private schools in any city those days did not have a fleet of school buses to pick up and drop the kids. It was not possible to send little children long distances by public transport. So the central school was a boon. The boys enjoyed and learnt how to live anywhere in our vast country along with a cross section of children from all corners of India belonging to any caste, creed or faith. They could learn more languages to speak at least. The standard of education was quite high. I think children by themselves are a happy lot who just want love, good food, a little freedom and lots of fun.

Pallankuzhi (Mancala)

Carrom board, 'chaupar', the game of dice, Paramapada Shobhana Padam (Snakes and Ladders)

Chess a game which originated in India

Caption: ' Hop, Skip and Jump, a wonderful outdoor game of our era'

04

No Dearth of Entertainment

Today we come across nuclear families and that too with just one child or two children at the most. But our childhood was spent in nice huge families. I feel it was a blessing.

It is not easy for us seniors to accept changes, but as children we were able to adapt to various lifestyles. We learnt to live with uncles, aunts and cousins as we had a huge extended family.

Any distant relative on a visit to Madras would just land unannounced in our house with a cast iron trunk, cotton pillows rolled in bedsheets, cloth bags, and a tiffin carrier. My parents welcomed the guests with broad smiles and open arms. Within minutes my mother would bring glasses of coffee and help them to settle down in the space available. In all probability there would be other guests already in our house.

"You can sleep in this big hall. We can adjust, no hassles", my father would tell them with a broad smile. We children took it as our way of living.

Besides a radio and the oldest model of gramophone which were our source of music and entertainment, there were only board games that we kids could play. In fact when my cousins brought a view master from England with 3 dimensional fairy tale slides, I watched in complete awe. I had not seen an image three dimensional! We only had the unforgettable HMV records of the early days of recording. One was 'Rukmini Kalyanam' a Kathakalakshepam, M.K.T.' Bhagavathar's film songs and D.K. Pattammal's Bharatiar songs, MSS' songs from the film 'Meera' etc. which we could play on the gramophone. But our good old gramophone would die every ten minutes. The key had to be wound. While winding, it would unwind and hit back the fingers in the reverse direction.

If we went out it was to the beach mostly. The beach has been our all-time favorite and ultimate choice for an outing in the stuffy weather of Madras, especially in summer. We sometimes took a ride in the tram. It was a short and sweet ride. The most delightful and thrilling experience was standing along the shoreline at Santhome or Marina beach, getting drenched up to the knees in the waves lashing in all heights and directions. Back home after the visit we would happily deposit all the sand we collected on our feet, legs and dresses on our floors. Our mother must have had a tough time cleaning up the mess.

The peanuts we bought on the beach obviously cost peanuts. The sliced mangos with red chili masala sprinkled on them made our eyes and noses run and the droplets fell on the slices. We were dripping from every orifice on the face, but we wanted more spices on the slices.

In cities like Madras by the mid 50's we had quite a few auditoriums where we could watch historic stage plays put up by professional troupes and satiric and humorous ones put up by amateurs in Tamil. We could enjoy live Carnatic music concerts and dance performances held in airy open air theaters with thatched or asbestos ceilings and side walls made of woven bamboo mats.

There were one or two air-conditioned auditoriums in the city. Back then several sabhas were constructing their own premises but they were not operational as yet.

We enjoyed watching the circus at least once a year. It was a unique show with exciting trapeze acts and thrilling stunts with bikers and cyclists. Magicians, clowns, acrobats, and jugglers performed a lot of tricks. Lions or tigers jumped through rings of fire. Elephants sat on tiny stools. Monkeys did monkey tricks. It was said that cruelty to animals was one reason the circus had to see the end of its life. It is said that the poor animals were hit hard to be trained to perform in front of a crowd day in and day out. These animals and hundreds of artists and trainers had to be accommodated, fed and transported from place to place. That must have been a marathon task for the circus companies. But now it is fast becoming a thing of the past. It was a great action packed live show, no doubt, but perhaps it was not patronized much.

When 'circarama' came to Madras our father took us of course.

Another popular show was the thrilling magic by magicians like P.C. Sorcar, Virgil and several others. A live show used to be absolutely riveting. Nothing on thc scrccn can cqual that thrill. Remember we did not have television shows of circus or magic or any such thing then, but the live shows were fantastic. We had not heard of television then.

Cricket test matches were played in Madras every winter in the 40's and 50's. The rest of the year there were no other series like One day matches consisting of 50 overs for each team or the T20 series wherein each team gets only 20 overs to prove their cricketing skills. Since the weather was quite warm the rest of the year in India, there were no matches organized during the other 8 months. They were played only during winter and there were only test matches played lasting for five days. My brothers, brother-in-law, and cousins, friends were all crazy after cricket. It was a great treat for me given by my brothers, that too when I came to high school. They agreed to take me along to watch it live only one or two days during a test match. Of course for this treat I had to learn what cricket was, the rules of the game, in short everything about the game including what was called a 'chinaman' bowling from my friend. I thank her even now. In the non TV era running commentary on the radio was the only way to know what was happening in Chepauk Stadium, Eden Garden or at Lord's stadium. My brothers had their nerves on edge on the final day of the match. They stood hugging the radio or even beat the radio set in excitement, while listening to Vizzy's running commentary. Ahhhh. He took his own time to give comments about the last ball when the boys wanted to hear what happened after the last ball was bowled. Those were thrilling days.

Exhibitions now known as Fairs gave us a gala outing. The next day we had helium-filled balloons stuck to the ceiling, soap bubbles floating all around, water filled balls broken on the mosaic floor, whistles, puzzles, black paper snakes and green frogs were strewn all over. New kitchen gadgets were added, but they worked only in the seller's hands. There were pavilions put up by railways, PWD, EB with working models. We stood in long queues to see them, but it was good with a lot of working models, lights and commentaries. It was informative and educational. My father insisted we see them all.

But most of the time in the exhibition someone had to stand in a spot and count the heads. It was very easy to get lost. A cousin of mine went missing once and how his father went round and round and then public announcement was done every fifth minute

“Hey, Babu, where are you, your father has been searching for you. Come to this office near the main gate immediately”. He was found after forty minutes. Then it was time to pack up and come home. Poor Babu was taken to task by all of us.

Oh, those were carefree days going out in groups to any event whether it was a wedding or a cinema.

But we were ever ready to go out. Even for gossip and small talk we would stand near the gate or near our fences or anywhere in the fresh air in complete harmony with nature, among trees and flowers. We loved life outdoors.

Ah, well, that was a different era.

Team 11 of India playing a Test match

Old Gramophone-our only source of music

05

Heavy Metals Rocked at Home

It was the late 40's and early 50's. The earliest that I can recall of my mother's kitchen is roughly this period. A heavy cast iron stove called 'kumutti aduppu', 'chullah' in Hindi was on the cement platform. Circular shaped like a deep frying pan with a grilled plate in the center to hold the charcoal, it stood with the burning coal pieces. On this uneven surface it must have been a huge task balancing heavy brass utensils. This was the main stove my mother used. I don't know how my tiny mother who was just 4 '8 "in height managed!!

There was another semicircular iron frame with an opening in front to hold the logs in place. It was no better. The logs had to be pushed, pulled and prodded with a brass flute-like contraption. A hand fan was used to make them catch fire. One minute they would burn like forest fire in California and next minute they would die to become a tiny flicker. There was a chimney lined with soot in the corner right above the platform with 'Chulha'.

My mother had kerosene stove which needed pumping. It was literally like playing with fire. It made a lot of scary noise. Those days brass utensils with the 'kalai' lining done inside with tin or lead or whatever metal alloy, were used for everyday cooking. The lining was a must otherwise the brass could cause food poisoning as it would react with tamarind, lemon juice or anything acidic. If there is no tamarind there is no South Indian cooking. How did my mother manage?

The 'kalai', tin lining is called 'lead lining' 'Eeyam poosaradu' in Tamil, called for technical expertise. A person used to come once in a while with all his paraphernalia to redo the 'kalai 'lining'. He would set up a mini foundry on the street with open fire, a billowing bag to pump some air, a melting hot metallic liquid in a crucible and spread it evenly inside the utensil. But thinking back I feel he had a tremendous skill in his hands.

The heavy utensil called 'vengalapanai' (bronze pot') did not require this lining. It was the favorite pot to cook rice. For the harvest festival called 'Pongal', like millions of others, my mother too made 'sakkaraiPongal' (the sweet rice with jaggery) in one such pot. We were asked to standby to beat a metal plate with heavy spoons and shout 'Pongalo Pongal' when the milk was boiling over putting off the fire underneath. It was fun. Milk boiling over was considered auspicious. Millions celebrated the festival like this outside in the fields under the sun. This Pongal was offered as 'naivedyam' to Sun god.

There was no sink in the kitchen but a faucet was there for the corporation's water supply. We used to drink the water coming from that faucet. It was filtered with a thin white cloth and collected in the brass pots called 'kudam'. Earthern pots were filled with water to keep it cool as Madras remained and remains mostly hot and humid. We did not use water purifiers at home nor bought bottled mineral water. People trusted the treated water supplied by the city corporation. But a few years later when my eldest brother became a doctor we became very aware of germs and microorganisms and saw them floating and flying all around.

Amma was told to boil and cool the water to drink. Was ignorance bliss? Today we need to pass water through carbon filters, semi permeable membranes, ultraviolet rays, in short RO it, whatever that means.

Hey, we were not falling sick all the time in our childhood!!! After all I am eighty and living still.

Besides brass utensils Amma used deep cast iron pans for frying and flat iron 'Tawas'(pans) to make dosas and roti's, which we called "chapattis". Any pancake could be made on these flat pans. There were a variety of them made with rice and some lentil or the other in various permutations and combinations. A Rukmini cooker entered our kitchen before the pressure cooker did. In this brass container dal and rice could be cooked at one setting. Every housewife bought it. It was considered a great invention.

"Kalchatti" was smooth soft stoneware, my mother and millions of others used to make Sambar in. The stoneware was preferred for making 'Vatral kuzhambu', a spicy liquid made with dried berries in tamarind sauce or 'morkuzhambu' a side dish made with coconut, green chilies and sour curds. Any vegetable in gravy with mixed vegetables and lentils prepared in South Indian style could be made in 'kalchatti'. There was some sort of competition as to who can cook the best 'vatral kuzhambu'. None was ready to part with their seasoned stoneware. My mother, mother-in-law and women of that generation used a piece of thick towel to handle the hot utensils on the stove with great expertise. The pair of tongs could not be used for these heavy and smooth cookware. On the other hand I could not handle the piece of cloth to bring any hot stoneware or cast iron pans from the stove. Many times I had to quickly throw a burning piece of cloth to save myself from catching fire and going up in flames..

I must mention the 'Eeyachombu' a white lead pot that was declared to be the best for making "rasam" by the connoisseurs of South Indian food. Let me be honest. As a novice I could not manage it on the gas burner as it started melting and got misshapen with burnt rasam sticking to the bottom. "It could not be pure lead, must have been tin, not lead", said my daughter-in-law, when I narrated the 'eeyachombu' incident to her. It seems the melting temperature for lead is very high. Whatever the metal was, it definitely passed on a special flavor to the rasam. Between you and me someone told me that the professional cooks those days dropped a lead pot in the rasam when they cooked rasam for hundreds of guests to be served in a wedding feast. Could it be true? It seems that it was to enhance the flavor of rasam. Don't quote me please when you tell anyone this secret.

In the 50s most of the middle class bathrooms had a copper boiler on an iron stand. This was used to heat the water for bathing. It was tough to get it started but boys enjoyed lighting it as they could burn newspapers and other fibers etc. Alternatively aluminum pots were used in millions of households as it would heat up water or anything else faster and it was cheaper and lighter to handle. They were tougher to clean though. With a million dents in the rounded bottom an aluminum 'degchi' looked like the moon with craters when it was turned upside down.

Copper and silver utensils were used for storing water in smaller quantities. It is said that many types of microorganisms and bacteria cannot survive in copper and silver containers. That explains why the holy 'theertham' in temples is kept in silver containers to which they add edible camphor and saffron too. Silver plates, glasses and cups were used in daily life by the middle class people, more for this health reason. Perhaps the silver was given to the bride as a part of the dowry along with jewelry in gold. Maybe middle class parents gave their daughters a couple of silver plates and glasses, at least whatever the cost was. It must have been a question of prestige too.

The kitchen had earthen pots, ceramic jars with screw type lids for salt, tamarind, pickles and even curds. Masala containers in wood were a must in the kitchen. The leftover cooked rice soaked in water from the previous night was consumed in the morning with salt and buttermilk added to it. It was said to be very healthy by our elders and most of the children had it as brunch before they left for school. It is a rich source of vitamin B12, say the researchers today. Is that so? We accept it as gospel truth now that it comes from research papers.

The families lived mostly on freshly cooked hot food which was boiled, steamed, sautéed, roasted or deep fried. Up north they used tandoor to make their heavenly flatbreads. People ate ice creams, breads, buns, biscuits and pastries but they were not homemade. There were huge bakeries making and selling them. Pizzas, pastas, noodles, burgers, burritos and tacos were I think not heard of, not even in urban India. There were no refrigerators to freeze the food and microwave ovens to warm them up as a rule in millions of households.

To sum it up, not only did the Bronze Age continue to be seen in the houses even the Stone Age implements were kept in the kitchens 80 years back. Grinding Stone with a rolling stone to grind for 'dosas' and 'idlis' was in a corner.

A flat rectangular stone with a rolling stone in yet another shape for grinding chutneys and masalas was on a platform to stand and grind. A pair of rotating round stones with a wooden peg hammered in was used to powder any grain was left somewhere for emergency use. The mortar and pestle were so huge and heavy that one had to stand and pound. It could mincemeat anything kept underneath. Our mothers' kitchens had them all some 80 odd years ago. The beauty is that they could handle them all till the age of 60 or 70. They must have had all the joints in working order, no doubt.

A decade after independence a gas stove was introduced. My mother could at last bid goodbye to the 'chulha', firewood and charcoal. They were out from the urban kitchens. Stainless utensils replaced the last pieces of expensive brass, bronze and silver. Though it did not have a gram of silver, it was called 'ever silver' in the south. The brass and bronze were worth their weight in gold as they had high resale value. Once sold, the home maker could fill the kitchen shelves with stainless steel utensils with the money they fetched. For the first time even utensils were sold on the streets. They were not only delivered at the door but also seemed free as there was no currency involved in the sale. 'Old clothes' changed hands yielding place for new sparkling cookware'. That was the exchange programme.

In many elite homes for guests it was ceramics, glassware, Pyrex and Corning ware on the dinner table but we middle class were happy with our stainless steel ware.

The last but not the least to revolutionize all households in the world and in our country was the introduction of plastics. The bathrooms got rid of zinc buckets and brass 'chombus' and got plastic buckets red and blue in colour. Copper boiler vanished and a water heater was fixed on the wall. The age old Horlicks bottles and 'Bournvita' tins disappeared from my mother's kitchen shelves to be replaced by colorful plastic containers. The plastic basket to store potatoes looked bright and clean but it is going to live forever till I decide to throw it in trash can and it will live there in the heap of trash for eternity.

The kitchen was the kingdom of every mother where she reigned supreme. She dished out two to three square meals besides varieties of beverages for 10 to 20 members of a family. How she managed in smoky kitchens, and how she could grind for idlis, dosas and chutneys without electric mixers and grinders. It is a wonder how she kept the supply chain going and she smiled after all these?

We did not even celebrate her ever. They did not have a Mother's day, but every day they knew she was their best friend. We were taught in school, "Matru Devo bhava, Pitru Devo bhava, Acharya Devo Bhava and Atithi devo Bhava", meaning mother, father, teacher and guests are to be treated like gods.

Amma's Kitchen replicas from Bronze & Stone Age

Kumatti Aduppu (Chulha)

06

Life in a Village

Bullock carts were a popular mode of transport for people in our country till about a hundred years back, especially in the villages and small towns. In the cities and bigger towns there were horse drawn carts. These were called 'jutka vandis 'and in Madras these were seen outside the railway stations, bus terminals, temples and hospitals. I have seen a lot of 'jutka vandis' in my childhood and by the 50's perhaps they went out of use as they could not be seen much.

The bullock carts were in extensive use though they took a long time to cover even one mile. After our marriage when we went to his village my husband promised me he would give me a taste of a bullock cart ride.

He was looking for a chance. It came when we both had to go to a nearby temple in his village. The temple was not very far off, but not exactly a walkable distance. It was decided to go by a bullock cart for the fun of it. But I must say, it was painfully slow. The bullocks seem to be highly temperamental. All of a sudden they refuse to move.

It was then that my husband was reminded of the rides he had taken with his cousins in his childhood. It seems the cart in which he traveled in the early 40's, took 3 hours to cover a distance of

14 kms from his native town to his uncle's home in the village. He said the passengers, he and his young cousins took the painfully slow bumpy ride in their stride without grumbling. Buses were not very regular in that route and even if they came they were not much faster. It seems a trip by bus on muddy roads used to be more rattling and shattering than a ride by bullock cart. The boys sat back and enjoyed eating super soft 'Jasmine like idlis' (a famous expression of Tamilnadu' to describe the softness and whiteness) smeared with sesame oil, chutney powder with a thick coconut chutney by the side.

My husband said as young boys they did not fret and fume about discomfort in the vehicle or the terrible condition of the roads. They enjoyed the ride thoroughly, singing, which was more of shouting, some film songs in chorus. The hero in the film would have sung this song riding in a bullock cart chasing the girls, plucking tamarind pods from the roadside trees. The boys had the cart to themselves as their mothers were in a different cart. They could relieve themselves of any pressure in the bladder by the side of the roads in the open fields, washed their feet and played in the cool streams flowing by the road side in some place. These kids had simple demands and they were happy with simple pleasures.

I thought it must have been a lot of fun. They knew that a grand feast awaited them at their destination in their uncle's house. His uncle and aunt lived with their own children and their brother's children as well. It was a large joint family.

It was not fun for the women of the household though. But in all probability, they were used to that lifestyle. Perhaps they had no time to think even as they must have been busy from dawn to dusk. They had a farm where they cultivated bananas, coconuts, tuvar dal and some vegetables too. They had paddy fields a little distance away. There were a couple of cows in the cowshed in the backyard. Sivakasi, the town nearby, had power supply, but there was no electricity in the village. The family would finish their dinner early and go to bed after cleaning up the whole kitchen. Even the kids had to get up early in the morning. The patriarch was the head of the joint family. He was a disciplinarian as all fathers used to be those days. He had a lot of administrative work to do.

My husband has vivid memories of his aunts and mother cooking together in the kitchen. Early in the morning womenfolk would have fought with wet logs to make them catch fire and cook the food faster. A flute-like contraption made of brass had to be used to blow air through to kindle and keep the fire going. The ashes would come flying from the dying coals and the smoke would surround them. First of all they had to sit on the floor and cook. They would cook only after taking a shower before sunrise by the side of the well. They had to draw water from the well, by dropping a bucket deep inside and pulling it up carefully without spilling the contents. Wrapped in a sari, pouring cold water from the well in the early morning with the nip in the air must have been very uncomfortable.

The bathroom would be close by, but it was just four walls without a proper weather-proof roof. The roof usually was a tin sheet supported by wooden rafters. A flimsy door made of a tin sheet fixed on a wooden framework would have been there. The choice was to either take a bath before sunrise near the well or carry buckets of water to the bathroom and bathe. I had seen such a bathroom in my grandfather's house. Those houses in villages had just one huge bathroom and one toilet, irrespective of the number of people living there. Menfolk and boys as a rule bathed by the well side. Little boys did not mind sharing the toilet too, if nature's call was urgent. Toilet was just 3 and 3/4 walls, one quarter kept open as an entrance. A bucket at this point meant the toilet was 'occupied'. Most of the villagers went to the open fields to answer nature's call. Even this sort of 'private toilet' with a 'bucket watch' was a luxury those days.

After the era of the bullock cart came the horse-drawn cart. I have enjoyed riding in horse-drawn carts a few times in Salem. The body of the cart was almost similar. It neither had steps to climb nor cute windows and curtains to peep through. There was just one square piece of iron step and someone from inside the cart gave a hand for the co-passenger to get onto it. There were no majestic white steeds to pull the coach like the royal carriage had which we get to see on television. It was not the buggy you see in Clint Eastwood's Wild West movies either. This horse drawn cart was a small buggy with two huge wheels, a wooden base covered with some hay and a worn out cotton sheet to sit on. Hay and dried grass could poke through the cloth. The body of the cart was built with wooden side walls and a cloth covered bamboo framework which acted as the roof for protection from sun or rain. A single horse pulled the cart with much poking and prodding by their owner. Three adults and two kids could sit with folded legs. I guess the driver took one look at the size of the passengers and decided who would sit where after weighing them mentally. Then he would sit in the front to nudge and whip the horse to make it embark on its journey.

He would shout at any passenger who shifted his/her bottom upsetting the delicate balance. He did it without turning his head to see who did it. When you reached your destination you had to gingerly put one step down on the tiny square piece of metal at the back again and then another step on the ground. One hasty step, would lead to a nasty fall on the road. I must say it was an exciting experience. The bus service was there but the complaint was the same. The service was infrequent and irregular in that route.

The cart which we came across on our city roads in our childhood was the hand-pulled rickshaw. It was followed by a cycle rickshaw, which was a lot better than the hand-pulled one as the cycle could be pedaled by the man who was manually pulling the rickshaw earlier. The city of Madras had trams running in specified routes. We had taken rides in all of these. Next vehicle to be introduced in our country was the auto rickshaw which had an additional third wheel. People could travel slightly faster inside the cities. Soon the city roads saw more traffic with bicycles, autos, cars, buses, taxis and trucks running during the day. A few years down the line, the two wheelers became the most preferred vehicle for all the youngsters and even men in all age groups. To start with in the 50's there were not many women riders but they joined the menfolk a decade or two later.

The suburban trains started to run to facilitate people to travel from the suburbs to the city proper to work and commuters to go from the city to the suburbs to their factories or back to their homes. Cities like Bombay, Madras, Calcutta and Delhi had these trains started operating from the '20s or even much earlier in some places.

Our long journeys across the country in the 60's and 70's were mostly by trains, which were hauled by a steam engine or two. Then came the diesel engine and finally the railways started the electrification of the tracks. The electrification went in separate stretches and now it is reported that the electrification process is 100% complete. India has one of the longest networks of railway lines. There are around 13,500 passenger trains transporting millions of passengers, moving between 7340 stations covering a distance of 1,23,500 kms every day. These are the figures I saw on the Internet. Amazing!!! Besides these passenger trains, it seems, there are goods trains which earn most of the revenue for railways. In short, today Indian railways is one of the most efficiently run organizations in the world.

We have travelled in every type of coach including unreserved 3rd class compartments to 3 tier, 2 tier, a/c two tier, a/c three tier, a/c first class, a/c chair cars, double decker's and even in a railway saloon, buying tickets of course. But the puff and huff of the fascinating steam engine remains etched in my memory. It had an old world charm all its own. We have fast moving trains today like Gatimaan, Shatabdi, Rajdhani and the latest is 'Vande Baharat Express' which can go at 180 kms per hour.

We have flights operating 24x7 from around 200 airports in India. The distance we covered by train in 2 days (48 hours) is covered by a Boeing in two hours. How lucky we are to have travelled by bullock carts to Boeings in a single lifetime.

But it is said that millions of bullock carts are still used in rural as well as urban India as they can haul heavy loads even on muddy and narrow roads. They still remain a mainstay of transportation in today's India. Farmers use bullocks not only for plowing but also for moving harvested crops, weeds, manure and other essentials. It is said that some freight might be carried by jet aircrafts but for the last few miles people still use bullock carts. We do come across such carts on our highways bringing the entire traffic of colossal container trucks, sand Lorries and fast moving high-end cars, to a crawling speed. But bullocks are cool; they don't seem to get flustered. They continue moving at their own speed very casually.

It is so interesting to watch!!!

Typical sights in a village

Village Gossip!

07

Entertainment in a Village

Life in a village, which my father and uncles experienced as children, was not the same as in big cities and towns. My uncle, who saw more of village life for a longer period, said the street play called ‘therukkoothu’ which the villagers presented used to be very interesting and entertaining. He was telling us about a real life incident which happened in a village near Pattukkottai. In that context the talk turned to ‘therukkoothu. It seems the ‘koothu’ was staged on a wooden platform erected in the open where a lot of people could assemble and watch. The audience had to sit on mats and durries.

It was a prolonged overnight show which would commence after sunset and would go on almost till sunrise. It had long and loud soliloquies. Every actor would render his long rhetoric at the highest decibel level in Tamil. Some sort of mike was there sometimes but they did not need one. The plays were melodramatic, the stories being based mostly on our epics Ramayana or Mahabharata. Actually the epic Mahabharata was a treasure house of stories for the playwrights to draw inspiration from. Till today it remains a storehouse of tales for authors to get inspired from. India has had a long history as it is thousands of years old. The tales were sometimes about heroic kings and queens of the past. The plays had songs back to back and actors who could sing were very popular. Playback was unknown then.

Actually the funniest part was that men played female roles. My uncle saw 'Keechaka Vadam' (the killing of Keechaka) by one of the Pandava princes, Bheema. The role of Draupadi was played by a male actor. He acted well, but his voice gave him away. With a lot of makeup, bushy eyebrows (thankfully, he had shaved off his mush), fake jewellery, colourful costumes, anklets and his gait, though not very graceful, he looked like a woman but the voice was gruff. Our uncle even repeated the dialogues and he sang also. It was funny the way he mimicked. The stage plays had songs back to back and actors almost danced across the stage. The dialogues were written well. Generally whatever the play was it was a meaningful story and mostly carried a message for the audience.

A few years later they came to be called 'natakam'. A lot of actors came from the stage plays to the silver screen in Tamilnadu. They became playwrights, super stars, comedians and villains too. A few who entered politics became chief ministers. The theatre must have been connected to social life of the people. It consisted of 'Iyal, Isai and Naadagam'. Iyal means literature, isai means music and naadagam is drama.

When movies were made initially they were silent movies. Dadasaheb Phalke was the first filmmaker to make a full length Indian feature film. It was a silent movie called 'Raja Harischandra', which was released in May 1913 in Bombay. It was a commercial success. He is said to have been inspired by the movie 'Life of Jesus' which he saw in 1906 CE. The first talkie to be released in the year 1931 in Hindi was 'Alam Ara' and in Tamil the talkie was 'Kalidas'.

These talkies were made and screened in the 'touring talkies' which were showed in tents. They used to be temporary structures. Audience who bought tickets for more than a rupee or two had to sit on benches and those who bought cheaper tickets had to squat on the durries. It was called 'tarai ticket'. Initially the cinema was a copy of drama with back to back songs. In general for us Indians music and dance are an essential part of our lives. I think music runs in our genes and it does not end with singing in the bathrooms. Little wonder our films are full of them. India has a rich collection of folk songs in many languages. Folk dances are any number and each region had a rich repertoire of dances with colourful costumes, masks and accessories.

Hey, I have seen a movie once in a 'touring talkies' with my uncle's family. I was a ten or eleven year old girl. The cinema was shown in a tent. The 3 hour show went on for more than 4 hours as it had numerous intervals and breakdowns due to power cuts or for changing reels in the projector. Whenever the film got cut, the audience would whistle loudly. The soda vendor would start selling his coloured drinks, walking around among the audience, hitting their legs with his partitioned wooden 'bottle carrier', shouting 'soda, colour, biscuits,' beating the bottles with the metal opener in his typical style. By the way 'Colour' was a coloured soft drink, God knows what sort of concoction it was and what colours they used. I hope they were some edible colours.

Coming back to our visit to touring talkies, we were reaching the end of a not-much-known Tamil cinema, when the tragedy struck. In fact I did not remember the name of the movie. The power went off due to a sudden downpour. The restive audience squatted close to the screen on a worn out durrie, perhaps, could almost touch the screen. They must have paid 2 annas per ticket (12 paisa) they started whistling and walking, creating a ruckus. My uncle brought us all out hurriedly. Till today I wonder what happened to the heroine in the end. Did she marry the hero or was she killed by her family? The story was somewhat like Romeo and Juliet's love story. The trouble was I forgot the name of the movie. I could never find out how it ended. In the end the Tamil movies they always showed 'Subham 'at the end, which means the end was auspicious or happy. Somehow the end would be made happy too as the tragedies were not welcome by the audience those days.

Did that cinema have a happy ending?

Theyyam: Folk dance of Kerala

Ayyanar guardian of a Village.

08

Weddings of Yore

When I was in my pre-teens and teens, I remember I was busy attending a lot of wedding celebrations of my siblings or one of my cousins or children of our family friends, especially during summer vacations. We used to travel by car or train inside Tamilnadu or to a city or town in nearby Karnataka. In our family my sister's wedding was the first to be celebrated. And the venue was just across the road. Our house was full with guests. I was a small girl just enjoying the sweets and snacks made at home in large quantities by professional cooks.

But a few years later my eldest brother's marriage was in Srirangam in the peak of summer in the small island town near Tiruchirappalli. We had to travel by train and that meant a lot of fun for us. A lot of our extended family members gathered at Egmore station to embark on our train journey. After all the fighting for window seats and upper berths, we kids and teens were asked to sleep on the durries spread on the floor of the carriage. Early next morning, maybe 50 of us ranging in age from 7 weeks to 70 years landed at Srirangam station. The venue of the wedding was a huge heritage type of bungalow and we were to stay in a bungalow nearby.

The groom's party, that's us, called 'sammandis' were taken to the bungalow where we were to stay. We were greeted by the bride's parents, uncles and aunts. As soon as we entered, the young mothers with babies in arms started looking for hooks in the ceiling. I think they walked in with eyes fixed on ceilings. Soon three or four cloth cradles were seen hanging like cosy little hammocks in which babies were being rocked by their mothers. Within an hour there were puddles of watery liquids underneath every cradle. If any aunt found the baby crying, she would rock it to make her/him go back to sleep. The young mothers had to keep an eye on their mischievous toddlers too. We really had a lot of kids in our family in all age groups.

Well, it must have been a lot of work for the bride's parents to look after the boarding and lodging of 50 odd guests with mischievous boys and infants on one side and old people on the other side for 4 days. But it is said that those days it was the custom for the groom's family to go to the bride's hometown for the wedding. No wonder a middle class couple with lots of girls had deep furrows on their foreheads and they looked perennially worried.

At bedtime elderly people in our family found a place under the fans to stretch their limbs. The few cots provided in the rooms were occupied by the privileged few. There was a huge durri, called 'jamakkalam' spread on the floor with a number of pillows on which women and kids slept. Menfolk and boys were in another room with the same bedding arrangement. Girls were with women. It was so simple. None went in search of a room in a hotel or complained about the accommodation. The families were bonding better, literally sharing bed sheets and pillows. Were they sharing lice????

Next morning for toilets and bathrooms there was a queue. Men and women generally waited for their turn, cracking jokes, chatting in groups standing with towels on their shoulders and soap boxes in their hands. People did not mind standing like that.

Younger lot went to the nearby river Cauvery for a bath. I heard later that they perhaps finished their morning ablutions on its banks. We girl cousins giggled when one uncle asked the boys directly.

When there were wedding celebrations some minor issues would crop up regarding food, accommodation, respect given etc. An uncle might remark,

'It' s all okay, but that man could have gone around with a second helping of Sambar and chips, at least, some appalams".

Some old aunt would say she was not greeted respectfully. Such minor things are bound to happen in an assorted group of people anywhere. But wise elders generally intervened, laughed and solved such minor issues.

There was a traditionally decorated 'pandal' in front of the house with banana plants on both sides of the entrance. There were 'Toranams' made of mango leaves with strings of flowers hanging in between. Huge rangolis in white outlined in red were drawn right from the road to the mandap inside. The groom and his parents, the bride and hers were kept busy doing rituals under purohit's directions. There were a number of brass pots called Kalashams. Next morning we found painted mud pots with white or yellow threads criss-crossing tied by the priests. There were two huge bronze lamps lit and kept throughout as in case of the power failure. I presume these oil lamps helped to see things in a better light, pun intended. Trays filled with things like coconuts, betel leaves, haldi, kumkum, bananas, blouse pieces, garlands and the famous jasmine flowers rolled up like huge balls were present morning and evening. This is a feature that got embedded in my brain as I saw them in every auspicious function and in every wedding photo in our albums.

My younger cousins and I decided to slip out to take a tour of the house on our own. A pathway led us to the hot kitchen that we dared not enter. We went behind where we saw huge fires flaring up from logs of wood in a longish pit. One man in a dhoti with a wet towel thrown on his shoulders was frying 'vadas' and another sitting next to him was stirring Sambar in a huge cauldron and the third one was scooping out steaming hot idlis and collecting them in a basin. Poor man, he was covered with sweat. A man very neatly dressed in a white dhoti, a shirt, and an angavastram on his shoulders, was giving orders all around. My cousin said he was known as 'head cook' and we had to address him as 'mama'. He is known as the 'master chef' today. We moved out quickly before this 'mama' could say anything to us. When we came back to the mandap priests were chanting mantras at a louder decibel level. Loud tinkling of bells could be heard. Some women were singing while 'aartis' were being taken.

After a few minutes we were having our idlis, vadas and Kesari In the dining hall. This was served on banana leaves and we had to sit on thin mats. Three times a day we enjoyed a different kheer, a different sweet and a generous helping of papads, chips, dry curries and gravies of sorts. I only wished I had my plate to eat on. Let me tell you at this juncture, eating on banana leaves is an art. I had to literally catch the rasam and Sambar from running all over the leaves. It was a huge task for me.

In the evening we all went to the temple. Some rituals were held there. My brother was seated in the centre with my parents sitting on his two sides. He was given a new suit. He had to change his dress. The rest of the crowd were busy chitchatting. Then there was a grand procession starting from outside the main entrance of the temple. It was called "januvaasam'. My brother, dressed in a blue suit looking handsome, was sitting in a decorated car surrounded by kids of all sizes. There were men walking in front of the car and women dressed in Kanchipuram silks walking behind the car. Actually this 'janavasam remained the same in almost all weddings we went to. A live band playing and leading the procession was a special feature in this wedding besides the Nadaswaram team. The procession took a very long time for a short distance. That was supposed to be.

My sister-in-law who received the groom back at the entrance of the decorated pandal looked gorgeous in a heavy blue silk sari with glittering gold jewellery. With dimpled cheeks and doe eyes the teenager looked so coy and beautiful. My parents gifted her grand silk sari and jewels once the couple walked in and settled on the plank. Our whole family sat down all around the bridal couple. We children were standing anywhere we wanted to stand. Then it was time for dinner. A lavish dinner followed of course.

Day 2 was the most important day.

I noticed from my young newly married cousins to elderly aunts in the room that we were staying, breaking their heads and consulting each other as to what they would wear. Women love dressing up in any wedding. They become so conscious of their looks. My oldest aunt was busy blackening her grey hairs with Kajal (eyeliner). A younger cousin was using the same Kajal 'eyetex', around her eyes, admiring it from every possible angle. She sprinkled and patted the white talcum powder on her cheeks liberally. Each one was taking turns to go to the mirror to look at her reflection.

All the girls had pigtails. Cutting the hair short was not common those days. Very few families down south allowed such fashions. Incredible it may sound to you my grandchildren. All girls were dressed in full length silk skirts and waist length tops. Younger ones were in frocks of course.

At the venue proper, the priests were chanting mantras holding a white silk dhoti between the bride and the groom. When the barrier was lifted, more mantras followed of course. The head priest generally had a resonating voice and the way he chanted the mantras with one or two more of his group, it sounded very impressive and authoritative. My young and beautiful sister-in-law was in a rather simple traditional yellow cotton sari, heavy jhumkas, gold necklaces and a thick rose garland. My brother, now dressed in traditional dhoti, was leaning in front of her holding the 'Mangal sutra', the yellow thread. My elder sister was behind the bride, (hey, why was my mom not calling me?). My sister and my brother were busy tying the three knots and there I was trying to squeeze myself in the midst of stout women to reach the spot. I had only a secondary role to play as a second and younger sister I knew. Was I not the supporting actress even, to tie the knot? I wanted to be at least on the spot.

The nadaswaram team were playing with all their strength and breath. The drummer beat the drum nonstop. There were shouts of 'Getti Melam, Getti melam'. This non-stop beating of the drums went on and on, till someone asked for change of tune. Soon we heard 'Anandam anandamayine', announcing to the gathering 'our girl Janaki has become a bride, and we are all happy'. Hey, this tune is the same in all weddings. The bride's name could be anything but she will be called 'Janaki', (the surmise was the groom was Lord Rama and the bride was Sita).

I was spotted by the bride's father. He asked me, "Ha, little girl, congratulations. There you are, did you get a new sari?"

"No, but I got a new sister-in-law and my sister got a new sari, "I said with a smile. He laughed. I did not wear saris then, I was in a silk skirt and top. This dialogue remained stored in my memory.

That evening there was a Carnatic music concert by a very popular stalwart singer called GNB. It was organised in a pandal erected in the same compound. It was a custom again to have a feast of divine music for the ears too on the wedding day. Some families had two concerts or more if they celebrated a five day wedding.

Day three was another homam and my sister-in-law got a black beaded chain with some more golden discs. The whole place was filled with utensils of silver and brass, gifts to the bride again. Sweets in different colours were there, including pairs of cones filled with sugar coated cashew nuts, sweet boondis, and 'manoharam' (a typical jaggery sweet) to be distributed to all guests. After the ritual my uncle and my brothers organised a variety entertainment. Songs were composed making fun of all close relatives and a humorous 'harikatha' about my brother, the bridegroom. This was done by my third brother who was a medical student. He was a very good performer and singer too. The gathering enjoyed the jokes immensely. It was a happy crowd in a mood to enjoy.

So the fun part of the celebrations for the young couple started. It was called 'nalangu'. This ritual was meant perhaps for developing an informal friendship between the bride and groom. The couple were to break roasted papads on each other's back. A dozen papads crumbled. They had to roll a coconut between them and the bride was supposed to snatch it from the groom's hands. My brother did not like to trouble the young girl. Most of the grooms did it for their young brides. So in the second round he gave up his stronghold on the coconut. Next game on the agenda was fishing for the ring. The couple had to put their hands in a utensil with water and pick the ring sitting at the bottom. The winner was going to boss over the partner in his/her married life. This was the usual joke by the uncles and priests surrounding the groom.

The families had more fun those days as they kept cheering their own girl or the boy whom they supported.

In the evening both the groom and bride were taken in a procession in a decked up open car. The procession was similar to the one done earlier. The procession went around Sriranganathaswamy temple. There was a lot of crowd standing in front of their homes to see the bride and groom. The whole town was around the temple.

In short, weddings in India were huge long-drawn joyous celebrations when the two families got to know each other well since they were in close touch for days together, not just a few hours. After all, the girl was going to live with an altogether new family for the rest of her life. It was an alliance between two families and it was a relationship to be nurtured.

Traditional Rituals in Hindu wedding.

Description of the pictures in the collage

1st top row a wedding procession of the bridal couple in a decorated car 80 years back

Top centre. The Oonjal ritual of a wedding celebrated 100 years back.

Top right, The groom announces his departure to Kasi, a ritual called 'kasi yatra' 70 years back

The 'januvaasam', the groom in a grand procession soon to arrive at the venue, 70 years old.

A concert by the Carnatic music stalwarts, a famous trio in the wedding pandal 70 years back.

The last one in the bottom row yet another ritual called 'Nagavalli'

09

Women's Education in our Era

Once the school final exams were over and I scored good marks my parents thankfully decided to send me to a 'girl's college' nearby to graduate. I was so excited perhaps as it meant in a few more years I will get my 'bachelor's' degree, that is BA. Perhaps I was dreaming that I could go on studying and then start my career like my brothers did. My elder sister was married as soon as she finished her school finals. I was lucky. I was going to enter the portals of the university.

I applied and registered for a 'bachelor of arts' degree in Carnatic music, as desired by my father. What I mean to say is, it was not exactly my choice but I had to listen to my father. I was learning Carnatic music and I liked to sing, but I wanted to study English literature in college. I thought music was my hobby. But my father had other plans for me. Unfortunately the girls' college close to our house did not offer English as the major subject to graduate in. Within the next few years they offered that choice but by then it was too late for me. And my father felt that it was the best college because of its proximity and it was very safe for the girls as they imposed a very strict discipline. According to him it was just a degree I had to get and since I was not going to take up a career, it was okay for me to learn more music and perhaps I should take music more seriously. That was that. I had no choice.

A couple of years later, for your information the college moved quite far from our home to new premises and I had to go by bus even to finish my graduation.

Anyway I had a wonderful time in college because my close friends from class 1 were going to major in music along with me and we would be together for four more years. Several other friends from my school joined the same college majoring in different subjects of course. For some reason in the first two years of college I remember girls from the same Alma mater used to stick together, just like they say 'birds of the same feather flock together'. We sat together in our favourite spot under a tree to have our packed lunch from home. Anyway in our college, there was no canteen or mess for the day-scholars to eat even one odd day. In short it was like we were back in the corridor of our old school.

We had to study and work hard of course. It was quite tough.

One was Shakespeare's most heart-wrenching tragedy 'King Lear'. The second was the bard's comedy, 'Much Ado About Nothing,'. Then there was the prose and poetry of Milton, Keats, Shelley, Wordsworth Robert Browning, Tennyson and some more. Sanskrit was tougher. Kalidasa's, Shakuntalam', a play in Sanskrit and 'Meghadutam', a poetic work by the same author and Dandin's 'Dashakumaracharitam' (prose) were hard to learn as we had to write long paragraphs and essays in Sanskrit. Kalidasa's descriptions of his heroines and Dandin's work too, were too romantic and their descriptions of women's torsos made us girls feel shy and feel embarrassed. We teenagers giggled quietly. Can you believe it? I presume, we lived in a different era altogether when all these topics were under wraps and never talked about in public. It was more so in a lot of conservative households. Even in cinema, romantic scenes were suggestive of the love between the boy and the girl invariably sang a couple of duets and ran around trees and plants but nothing more.

Carnatic music was taught in college but besides that a guru trained in a great parampara came home to teach me. Both the theory and the practical singing of classical music in all its intrinsic aspects were taught in college. Carnatic Music is an ocean, a boundless one. Perhaps as a student initially we could choose to enjoy standing on the shoreline where the waves come one after the other and we could get drenched a little. It was like getting a taste of various ragas and different types of compositions composed in them. We learnt several kritis, varnams, Padams, tillanas, javalis etc. by famous composers like the Trinity of Carnatic music and scores of others. Coming back to my analogy, we could walk a little more into the ocean, get a little wet in the slightly deeper waters, which can be compared to singing a short alapana and then sing the song. After that if we liked it, we could still go deeper into the sea, surf along a little or go deeper still surf-riding or try to sail across in a catamaran or go deep in a huge ship enjoying it immensely. This was like going deeper into learning when we had to delineate the raga, make our own Swara patterns, or do 'niraval' (singing the same line of lyric in several possible svara combinations and ways) and sing. There are those who just sit on the vast stretch of sand and enjoy listening to the music of the waves. They enjoy listening to music of other stalwarts. The choice depended on the love and dedication of the disciple of music. I wonder whether I was so deeply interested in music then but as I grew older and older I loved it.

For studying music to get our degree in classical music, we had to practise the detailed exposition of a ragam keeping in mind the particular combination of notes which formed that particular ragam. It called for a bit of manodharma (improvisation) or an intrinsic sense of ragas. We had to make several combinations of the swaras keeping the ragam and talam in mind and join it to the kriti at the right time and beat. That was called singing 'Kalpana swaras,' Even to explain it I find it tough. Readers can imagine how tough it would have been for me to sing. This is again the aspect wherein the manodharma (a capacity to improvise) of the singer comes out. The third was taking one line of the song, and singing it in different ways keeping the sahitya, ragam, talam and speed too in mind, not swerving out of any one of these aspects. I had to practise a lot at home to render 'ragam, tanam and pallavi' of a few major ragas for the final practical exam in front of a stalwart of Caranatic music to get my degree. My ancillary subjects were 'History of India' and "History and Theory of western music'. I even had to study a bit of Physics and Chemistry as minor subjects. It was a mix of unrelated subjects. We were not given an option to choose our own combination of subsidiary subjects or majoring in two different subjects etc. This was how the system was in the early 60's when we graduated.

Though not many parents were keen on their daughters taking up a career in our era, I mean in our generation, there were girls who wanted to become teachers, professors, doctors, nurses or learnt typing and shorthand writing to take up other administrative work in hospitals. Girls went on to do teachers training and worked in schools and colleges. Girls trained themselves to do secretarial jobs by learning typing and shorthand and were preparing to work in private enterprises or banks. But in general very few career options were open for girls then.

Compare it to today's scenario. Women have come a long way. They achieve a lot now. They are working everywhere in every position. Thankfully the world has changed a lot in these fifty to sixty years.

It is so wonderful to see women today in every profession including the administrative services, police services, and even working in investigative agencies like CBI, CID, NIA, though not in huge numbers. Women are in the political arena. In our country we have had a woman leading the country as the Prime Minister for nearly two decades. We have had a number of chief ministers and governors. We have a woman as finance minister now, who was formerly our defence minister. Ultimately we have had women as Presidents of the Democratic Republic of India. What more can Indian women ask for? Our country has actually proved its modernity and very equal treatment of both sexes by showing to the world that whether it is a man or woman, anyone who deserves and who could manage could occupy any chair in India. That much liberal our views are.

Women entrepreneurs are any number. Quite a few have an outlet for selling exclusive cotton sarees from home. A few run computers' classes or run a small software start up from home. There are homemakers, who take up production of papads, vadams and pickles at home. Women excel at multitasking too. They do catering service on a small scale. They can organise an event like a huge formal party or manage an event like a wedding celebration like the readers might have seen in the movie 'Band, Baaja, and Baraat'. They sell garments online which is a big business venture. Many teach music online. I have a granddaughter who is learning Bharatanatyam online and she enjoys it. A celebrity couple runs cookery shows online and their fan following must be in thousands. There are extremely successful lady architects and interior decorators and there are couples who are into this business in a big way.

The IT offices have plenty of girls working on computers as software and hardware engineers. There are women scientists in space research in our country. NASA has many women of Indian origin serving as scientists. Of course we have women scientists in ISRO too. Our NRI women get trained to be astronauts to go in the space shuttle and work in the international Space station. Kalpana Chawla, a woman of Indian origin went in one space shuttle to join the team in ISS but unfortunately met with a tragic end as the shuttle crashed. On alien shores women of Indian origin have held and are still holding high posts.

We have any number of women in the field of sports winning awards in cricket, badminton, tennis, wrestling, boxing, weight lifting in international sporting events. There are athletes, actors on stage, actors on the small screen, big screen, comedians giving live shows. In short we have shining stars in every field.

The percentage of girls joining the armed forces of our country is increasing year after year. To start with it was short service commission, but now they get much better deals. Finally girls have joined the Indian Air Force to become fighter pilots, which remained the last bastion to be conquered in India. They are flying fighters successfully. We can proudly proclaim today that our women drive any vehicle with ease from driving auto rickshaws on the busy city roads to flying 'Rafael' aircrafts high in the sky.

Hurray, I want to cheer them all up. The day my granddaughter gets a doctorate and another becomes a world famous author or playwright I will hold my head high.

In today's scenario girls can enter any field and reach the top. I am thrilled to see women achieve.

The author visits NASA

Woman Police patrolling

Women Scientists at Work

10

I Got Married One Fine Morning

Childhood and the carefree days, life in college as a grown up responsible girl to study and find out what I wanted to do with my life passed. Years just flew by. My father wanted me to get married and settle down. In fact the rule 'to settle down with family' was the same for boys too. They had to get married around 25 to 26 years of age or so. But they could study as much as they possibly could, choose the career they wanted, settle down wherever they liked to and choose the girl they liked best among all the alliances suggested by their parents.

After my eldest brother's wedding, within the next ten years the rest of my brothers got married one by one. They were all traditional arranged marriages and the celebrations were similar to the one in mode and manner as the one I have written about in a previous chapter. They were in different cities like one was in Mysore; another in Coimbatore and the last was in Madras. By then I was an adult helping in shopping and personally inviting hundreds of relatives and friends. Very soon our family had grown in size with several new entrants. The generation next to ours, the grand children of my parents started arriving. We were all not under one roof as my brothers lived in different cities and countries due to higher studies, job requirements but the new house my father built had a constant floating population. And we used to gather every summer invariably to celebrate some function or festival. What a memorable reunion it used to be. Huge families had this great advantage that when we met it was really a huge crowd in the house. My parents wanted it that way. That was the home where their grandchildren bonded with all their cousins, besides uncles and aunts.

Yes, my turn to get married came. One fine morning, in fact in the wee hours of the morning around 4.30 am, to be exact, I became the wife of a Flt. Lt., an engineer serving I A F. I was nervous and anxious like most brides used to be in my era because we did not know either the boy or anyone in the family. This was the case in most arranged marriages except when a girl married an uncle or a cousin perhaps. You will agree with me that it is not the same relationship to be just 'cousins' and 'husband and wife'. Even for cousins it might have been tough to settle down as this was a different cup of tea altogether.

In the 'mandap' hundreds of eyes were focused on me and I had to be careful at every step that I took including the 'saptapadi', the 7 steps that I had to take by the side of the fire and several rounds around the sacred fire that I took along with my spouse. We had to get up so many times to stand, hold hands, walk behind, bend, sit and get up again, do one namaskaram to the crowd in general or someone in particular. It was like a drill. 'Move closer', 'look up' 'give your right hand', 'smile', commands were coming from not only Purohit and my mother but from several corners. It was something rather like a parade except the commander in this case was not just one but many.

I realized I was entering a different era. I was going to be a new member of a large family to begin a fresh chapter of my life. I must have been anxious. But later I found that was easy to get adjusted to as I myself had grown up in a large loving family.

We spoke the same language, the same version of Telugu spoken in Tamilnadu, which I can call Tamilugu. Our cuisine was the same; the recipes were almost the same, only spice level was slightly higher. The dress was the same. We all liked to laugh and chat a lot. I had young sisters-in-law and brothers-in-law to talk to. What more could I ask for?

I slowly got introduced to the members of his family. We went to the temple of the family deity in the village, which my husband had gone to as a young boy in a bullock cart. He went there many times, always in a bullock cart, not the same of course.

Since I had never taken a ride in a bullock cart. I expressed my desire reluctantly to him. That day we were supposed to go by the taxi in which we came. But my husband explained to his parents about my desire to go in a bullock cart. They were surprised but so sweetly they suggested that we both can go to the other Krishna temple by a cart as it was much nearer to the house. They knew that this temple of Kali, the family deity was quite a distance and the road was very bad. We did go to the Krishna temple in the afternoon and I had described in an earlier chapter.

Every day new members of the extended family were introduced to me in the village. If it was a young person, I just smiled but if he or she were older to me I had to fall at her/his feet to receive her/his blessings. All these were our customs and traditions. Maybe children of today or even young couples see such scenes more in Indian movies than in real life.

“Beta, bahu, Dadaji ka charan Choona aap dono. Unka Ashirwad lena”, the father would say and the son and bahu would prostrate at his feet. We believe in the power of blessings given by elders.

After a week of meeting new family members and visiting temples we had to start our trip to New Delhi.

The GT Express leaving Madras Central for New Delhi

11

Married to the Military

It was twelve days after my wedding. Grand trunk Express was about to leave Madras Central. My parents, brothers, sister, sisters in law were all there to see me off. The truth struck me that in another five minutes the train would leave Madras where I have lived all my life. Needless to say I was shedding copious tears like I did when my sister left me alone in the school in the midst of strangers on the first day of school. She told me that I have to spend the whole day in a new environment among strangers, but they were all nice children like me. But looking around, I refused to leave her hand. My feelings at this juncture in the Madras Central were almost similar. After all, I knew I was going to Delhi for a week or ten days. My husband had to re-join duty in his unit and then get ready for joining a course at Coimbatore, which would be for about three months. So I would come back to Madras again before going to Coimbatore. But now it was different, as I had to say bye for an era in my life, a carefree era!

Ugh...it was a crowded programme. I kept waving my hands through the window. My eyes were misty and I could hardly see or hear. The steam engine blew the 'boo.....m' horn, the guard blew the whistle and the train started moving with a huff and puff in a very leisurely way. A few minutes later the train picked up speed and I was going farther and farther away from my parents and the rest of my family.

I was lost in thoughts. The train did stop every now and then. The usual vendors calling out 'tea, tea' changed to 'chai, garam chai after a few hours. Dining car was supplying breakfast, lunch and dinner according to their schedules. The food was picked up from one huge kitchen in a big junction and then supplied to the passengers who had asked for the service. My husband was explaining all these details as he had been going up and down several times since he was posted to Delhi, a couple of years back. He had seen many of the passengers carrying their own idlis and curd rice and they would keep going with that supply for two days. That I had seen once when I went to Delhi years earlier in a 3 tier compartment. The second day of course the sour curd smell might fill the carriage, but home food was the best according to many. We had food from the dining car which was kept anywhere and everywhere in the pathway where people kept walking all the time. I presumed our immunity came from such periodic exposure and intake of germs and bacteria. We had to just pretend we did not see it at all.

We had my husband's uncle stationed at Nagpur and he came to see us lovingly with a load of goodies at Nagpur station. It was such a huge parcel that he gave us, which consisted mostly of sweets like milk burfis, laddus and salty snacks like hot 'pakoras' and 'murukkus', which could be kept for a day or a week even.

We reached New Delhi station after more than 48 hours to stay there with my husband's colleague for a short spell. There was a small party that this friend had organised in the officers' mess to welcome us, the newly married couple, especially me, into the Air Force family. Formal introductions took place. I smiled of course but it was a nervous one I think. Soon the drinks were served. And the men were taking hard liquor, which I could only guess as it was in a different colour, not my favourite orange or cola. My husband gave me a glass of coke. I remember I spilt a little on my new silk saree. Naturally I was more worried about it. My husband came and whispered not to fuss about the coke on my saree but just keep listening to the lady talking to me. I started feeling uncomfortable but I had to look comfortable. I turned and smiled at her.

For a girl who had only seen Kali mark drinks, Gold spot, lemonade and Coca-Cola, these drinks looked different. I had never seen hard liquor and such parties till then as my father's circle of relatives and friends were all teetotallers like him. I had never gone to any formal party like the one in the officers' mess. I had only seen movies like 'Devdas', where drunken men holding their bottles were shown in a different 'colour' (pun intended) altogether. That was all the whiskey, rum or whatever I had ever seen.

Most of the Tamil movies would portray a drunkard who would either beat or treat his wife very badly or a villain who would rape and molest. Devdas was better. He immersed himself in liquor in order to forget the girl he loved. But the drunkard portrayed in Indian movies was villainous and vicious. The scene used to be full of his loud evil laughter and screams of a woman. She would be running like a rat around the room holding on to the last bit of sari tucked in her petticoat. For some strange reason she would run around a cot in a bedroom. I never understood why she entered the bedroom in the first place. Jokes apart, at this party I did not see even the slightest indication of anything like that. I don't mean running around the cots, but nothing silly, foolish and unbecoming of a gentleman.

By the way, this was a small gathering but later on I had been to hundreds of parties. I never saw any such behaviour ever. Coming to men in uniform they were perfect gentlemen, very courteous, friendly and respectful. Some of them would keep standing for hours together chatting and laughing for no side-splitting joke. One or two would be found smoking a little distance away. In fact they followed etiquette to a T. After two more days we left for Madras again.

We were back in Madras and went to Coimbatore where he had to undergo a course. Three months in Coimbatore just flew by, what with our travelling in the triangle of Coimbatore, Madras, and Salem half a dozen times. In mid-winter we were back in 'Rajokri' in the outskirts of Delhi where my husband was posted.

The general lifestyle was very different from what I was used to. Having grown up in a conventional and conservative family as the youngest child, I had lived a cocooned life down South. I was worried whether I would learn to adjust to new surroundings. I am talking about the time when most of the people up north did not know much about the 'Madrasis' living south of Vindhyas. I did not know much about their culture either, except what I had seen in Hindi movies and what I understood from the little dialogue I could follow. I am talking about the 'pre-subtitles' era. I had friends from the north like Gujaratis, Sindhis, Punjabis and Saurashtrians who were settled in Madras for generations. They were as much Tamilians as I was. After all, I was a Telugu speaking girl, not a Tamilian by birth. I was not fluent in Hindi. Of course most of the officers' wives seemed comfortable speaking in English but they would slide into Hindi-speaking mode within minutes as they felt it was more casual and enjoyable. We all do that. In fact we do it unintentionally; it is a natural drift to something we feel very comfortable with, which is our mother tongue of course.

The married officers' quarters of our Air Force stations looked similar in layout almost anywhere in the country. Most of them were 4 in 1, like our first home in 'Rajokri', in the outskirts of Delhi. The house plan, the flooring, the furniture given, the fixtures including the wash basins, sink and commodes fixed were almost similar in structure and brand name too. The neighbours were always good, easy to access and ready to help. They kept offering tea and snacks. In fact there was an easy camaraderie between the families.

I fell in love with 'choley bhature', 'kofta', 'baingan bharta', 'aloo paratha' and the parties. I was introduced to a lot of these garam masalas only after my marriage. For the first time I realised coconut was not the only ingredient to add taste to vegetables, even ground 'onion and tomatoes' or 'adrak lassoon' (ginger garlic) paste can give a distinct spicy taste. Tamarind was not an essential ingredient in every gravy. 'Aamchur,' and 'anar daana' could replace tamarind. The spices and condiments used in the south were more of mustard, jeera, methi, pepper, hing and curry leaves, while the north had cloves, cinnamon, cardamom, red chillies and coriander dry and fresh as well. That gave a different flavour altogether.

Thanks to my friendly neighbours and parties in the mess I got introduced to all these masalas in everyday cooking.

The permanent quarters that were built for officers had garages of course but the garages had more of two wheelers than cars. A two wheeler, the Lambretta scooter entered my life, along with my husband. We roamed around happily in the biting cold weather of Delhi. A few months rolled by after our marriage. The day came when I had to look for a gynaecologist. One of our friends told us about this wonderful doctor couple, a paediatrician husband and gynaecologist wife. What better combination can we ask for? I started consultations with the OB-GYN wife and in due course ended up with visits to the paediatrician.

I went to my parents' house in Madras to deliver the baby as that was our custom and tradition. I stayed there for a few months thereafter. But when I came back with a five month old infant in the famous winter of Delhi, I required a paediatrician as the baby was hit by colds and coughs quite often. Our visits to the paediatrician continued as our little son got some loose motion one day, constipation the very next week or a rash sometimes. If the little chap sneezed twice in a row, we would rush to the doctor.

It was the two-wheeler, a Lambretta scooter which carried us across. I used to bundle up my baby boy in several layers of woollens and go by scooter. I trusted and depended entirely on my mighty engineering husband's driving skills. The city roads were jam packed with cars, buses, two wheelers, minivans, 'phut-phutis' and trucks. 'Phut-phuti' was the speciality of Delhi. It is an 'onomatopoeic' word; the sound the vehicle made became its name. We chose to go via the upper ridge road as there was not much traffic in that route.

We knew how to move around in Delhi, where to go to buy what we want. We liked the city in spite of the extremes of hot and cold weather. But unfortunately postings came whenever we were nicely settled in brand new quarters among a good circle of friends and a maid made for us. I would even have a few potted plants taking root in their pots. It came, I mean the new posting. So there we were packing up a cradle, a baby cot, a perambulator besides the rest of the 'bisterbori' (bedrolls and bags), mattresses, trunks and deal wood boxes. The posting was to the air headquarters in Delhi itself. It was a local move but it was once again to the temporary quarters in a famous colony located in Sector II, R.K. Puram.

But not even temporary quarters were available. Now another set of my husband's friends offered their houses for us to stay while they were on annual leave. We shifted 4 times in 6 months before our own quarters were allotted. But we fell in love with the historic Capital city, along with its goodies, the lichis, chilkojas, (pines nuts), the Sohan halwa of Ghantewala, Kala jamuns of Gole Market, khulfi of Karol Bagh, 'nonkhatai' biscuits and 'naans' made in our local bakery and tandoor oven in our shopping centre. Jan path, Palika Bazaar, Sarojini nagar and Ajmal Khan road became our favourite haunts, more than us, our guests from south. We had plenty of them visiting and staying with us. We played our own carom board tournaments with our friends in the colony. We had a lot of fun like children.

The months went by very fast. I had to board a flight in the month of August 71 once again to go to my parents' place. Our quota of 'We two, ours two,' was being taken care of. Our second baby, a baby boy was born by the end of September. He was a tiny two-month old when the Bangladesh war started on the 1st of December '71. The war ended thankfully in a fortnight. India won the war for the neighbour. An independent Bangladesh was born. Our country was not sandwiched between two chunks of Pakistan anymore.

But within three months after the '71 war my husband got posted to Calcutta closer to Bangladesh. I was back from Madras with my two kids along with my mother in Jan' 72. We had to pack and leave by March. It was an ear-marked house for his post in Barrack pore and like I told you we settled down in the house comfortably with a smart woman to help with my million chores. Our elder son was put in yet another school for his upper K.G. class, the third one in two years. I can't even believe how the 18 months went past. The two kids kept me very busy. But promptly the posting came

Our temporary quarters in R.K. Puram, New Delhi

12

Family Expands and so Do Travels

My husband was asked to report to his Alma mater in Bangalore for a 'merger 'course. It was like a home posting Bangalore being close to both our home towns. We were very thrilled but our close friend in Calcutta was rather upset and he wanted to travel with us sightseeing, at least up to Odisha. The trip he suggested was to important temples and beaches along the east coast before our departure for the garden city down south. My husband readily agreed to take his whole family in our tiny car. We were 8 heads in numerical count seated in our two door wonder.

We went sight-seeing in Bhubaneswar, Puri, and Konark for five days. We had an exciting time running from temple to restaurant and from there to our rooms to rest. We had to get to the beach to stand and enjoy getting drenched in the waves and in between try a little shopping too. Perhaps we were trying to optimise and tiring the children too. After Konark our friend took leave of us to get back to Calcutta by train as he had to re-join duty.

We moved on towards Madras. We had to break our journey for six hours in 'Chilakaluripet', not to sight see but to cool our b...s in some shade. It was to save our little boys from dehydrating as the atmospheric temperature at 9am in Andhra Pradesh was crossing 40 or 42 degree C. We were looking for a cool and shady place. Yes, found the shade. We had to stand with a couple of cows in the midst of cow's urine, dung and hay as the building was under construction. But there was no other shade to take refuge as such on the deserted highway. After stopping over for that night in 'Eluru', we reached Madras the next day, almost a week after we left Calcutta. It all happened more than 45 years back!

How relieved we were to reach our home at last. Touring is great but not with small children. We should plan keeping them in mind constantly. Travelling is fun provided it is in air conditioned comfort or in suitable weather conditions. Sunny days are welcome but we cannot be standing right under the scorching Sun throughout.

Food seems to play a very important role in our daily lives. Foodies should either learn to compromise or carry their own pots and pans and go in a caravan. In that case we may end up cooking and not sight-seeing. Be ready to eat whatever is available on the spot. We can enjoy sight-seeing only if we do not worry about eating all the time..

But after reaching home we were full of stories to tell people back home how magnificent the temples were, how beautiful and serene the beach was in Puri. We forgot all those minor issues and remembered only the enjoyment part of it. In between we had to tell them a different story that I was about to be swallowed by the powerful waves rising one after the other in quick succession in the Bay of Bengal at Puri. My husband and his friend somehow managed to pull me out. My family got very worried. Perhaps it was the way I narrated the incident with frills and thrills. Hey, even an ordinary life can be exciting and thrilling.

Coming back to our life in Air Force, we reached Bangalore on time for my husband to join the course. The five years in Bangalore were one of the best years we ever had with our families as we could visit them more often and they could come and stay with us. We had 3 wedding celebrations in my husband's family. Weekends saw us out as we had several family commitments and guests galore. We shifted four times before moving into our married officers' quarters in 'Jalahalli', called the hospital town earlier. It was the barracks that were built by the prisoners of WWII as a hospital for the injured British soldiers.

'It was a cremation ground earlier,' someone said.

"Don't worry. When we came here ten years earlier it was already a dead crematorium," said some others.

Anyway we had a peaceful stay and all our domestic help came from the settlement on the very spot. They had been living there for decades. No ghosts were seen by my maid Raji.

AFTC was the college in which all technical officers who joined the IAF were trained. There was a new batch of cadets entering every six months and a 'passing out parade' was held every 6 months. These POPs and a lot of VIP visits, huge parties and AFWWA activities kept not only the officers but even their lady wives busy all through the year. The boys' school, a branch of Kendriya Vidyalaya was close by. Our younger son joined his KG class in a small building where KV had the kindergarten classes. It was hardly a stone's throw from where we lived. I still remember our cute little son stopping near the gate every morning to remind me that I have to go to pick him back from class before the bell rang at noon. It remains etched in my brain. He did n't respond when the teacher called out his name while taking attendance as he did not know his official name. Can you believe it? He only knew the name we called him at home, which was entirely different. Poor 3 year old boy, it was our fault.

All the buildings in Jalahalli West were built by the imprisoned soldiers during the 30's and 40's and so they were very old but

Bangalore was nice and cool back then. The rooms were huge and airy and even without ceiling fans we could manage. After nearly 5 years of a happy spell we moved to live in a pasha in the midst of lush green jungle and wildlife in Assam. The boys were thrilled about the move as their father had told them it was the natural habitat of leopards and black panthers. They thought it would be like visiting an African Safari Park on a holiday and didn't realise we would be there for months or years together.

Anyway we loved our stay in Assam as it was an entirely different experience to live in the midst of a typical 100% service crowd belonging to a small Air Force unit and a huge mountain division of the Indian Army. We lived in complete harmony with nature surrounded by lush tea gardens, tall trees, wild grass, bamboo forests on one side and rich wildlife all around us from leopards and black panthers to elephants, snakes, monitor lizards and several creepy crawlies, we could not even identify. The crawlies like snakes and monitor lizards even visited us at home. Readers, you might get to share your bathroom with lizards but have you shared it with a plump 6 feet long monitor lizard? Yes, one morning a giant lizard jumped from the rafters right into the bathroom on our son's small bicycle parked in the bathroom. We always used the other bathroom. Hearing the loud noise I entered it and was shocked to see this strange creature looking like a close-shaven crocodile.

My ten year old son said it was an iguana. The cook from the Officers mess came, hit it once and carried it like a baby in his arms and went. He said coolly that its meat was delicious to cook and eat. Its end was imminent. I hope monitor lizards are not on the list of endangered species or extinct now.

Assam had every type of landscape. The mighty Brahmaputra we could see near Dibrugarh was like an ocean and the tea gardens all around reminded us of how generous nature is if you don't restrict her. The rains were incessant and the fungus growth in the cupboards was persistent. The culture was unique and the people were so gentle and quiet. In short Assam was beautiful. We lived along with other officers' families like a close knit family in the midst of the jungle. Oh, no. We had all the comforts a little distance away like Kendriya Vidyalaya for kids, a clean swimming pool, tennis court, cinema theatre, a bakery to supply fresh breads, buns and biscuits. Our children were also allowed in parties as they could not be left to fend for themselves in the 'pasha' in the midst of a wild jungle. Actually a snake entered our kitchen one morning uninvited of course. But the men who came could not locate it." I saw it enter a hole in the wall",. I told them. They promptly closed the hole and said it would die there. I had to sing "alvida" (Farewell) to the poor creature. I could not save it. We have seen plenty of them crawling by just a few steps down in the entire area.

We ladies of the air force unit were members of the army ladies club too. There were parties and celebrations galore. It was a huge gathering.

We were hardly 50 kms from the border of Burma, Myanmar now. 'Chabua', the last airport of India was about 13 kms. away. Dibrugarh, the last city and civil airport of India was around 35 kms from 'Dinjan'. 'Tinsukia', a town 14 kms away was the last train station of India. We had oil wells nearby at 'Digboi' and 'Dhuliajan'. Where else could we see the natural gas burning continuously as a safety measure to prevent more dangerous explosions in the oil wells?

Calling people over the phone living in the rest of India to speak to them called for a lot of patience though. Sometimes the call won't happen at all. There was no civil post office. It was only APO, an Army Post Office. Letters would take a lot of time to reach us.

But this tenure also ended in about 28 months in the midst of an academic year but the boys said they would manage to continue their schooling in Delhi. That was the beauty of Central School.

From Assam we went back to New Delhi once again like a 'Frisbee'. From Kamarupa to Indraprastha we went, unlike Arjuna who went in the reverse direction from Indraprastha to Kamarup. It was to a different Air Force station this time. We were happy as we knew Delhi. It had changed considerably. We started with our stay in the officers' mess as usual and progressed to another two bedroom one and finally our own allotted quarters after 18 months. It had a nice backyard where the officer who stayed before us had grown a lot of vegetables. That inspired us. Soon we had 'aloo pyaz, bhindi, bhaingan, beans and beets' from our garden. We had our boys going to school 10 or 12 kilometres away in a school bus driven by their 'kind uncle' 'thavu', whom we all still remember. We saw movies galore in the open air theatre with several breaks like the good old 'touring talkies' of the past, which I had described in an earlier chapter. It was fun as the boys could run home for dinner or restroom break in between. The latest flicks of Big B donning the roles of an angry young man, we could see sitting under the starry sky. If it rained we had to go home. Everything was fun for the boys and naturally their joy was ours too.

In the midst of all these I did my master's in English Literature through a correspondence course. My father gave me all the support by sending me text books and redirecting the notes sent to his address by the university to our APO. He kept encouraging me with his affectionate letters. He saw to it that I finish my post-graduation successfully. As he did not let me do it when I was 20, he helped me do it at 40 so I did realise my dream after all. He was thrilled when I got my degree. I was in tears looking at his enthusiasm and happiness.

Every now and then I would remember the JEE notes from two different tutorials we got for our elder son lying unopened in a cupboard, but I was no tiger mom nor was his dad a tiger. The two boys were the playful tiger cubs growling and grumbling. They took JEE exams rather lightly and we parents could not force them to work10 hours a day.

A couple of years rolled by. We were in Delhi when our PM at that time met her tragic end at the hands of terrorists under unforeseen and shocking circumstances. The capital was shaken, as it faced uncontrollable riots and it sent shock waves throughout the country. Days' later life limped back to normalcy but it was not easy for those who witnessed the tragedy or saw the city in the aftermath to ever forget the tragedy. An uneasy calm prevailed for a long time.

We moved on to yet another posting on my husband's promotion to yet another part of Delhi. For the first time we stayed in the heart of the capital in the SP Marg complex located between two 5 star hotels. It was a nostalgic moment for us when we went there with our younger son and his family years later.

Well, let me continue my narration of the past. The elder boy could join a college in Dhaula Kuan, to do his graduation in electronics. He could just walk across to his college while the other boy had to go quite far to his school, but as I told you; we adjusted, always had to. Lots of guests, lots of going out as tourist guides, lots of cooking I had to do, but + points were we had an attached servant quarters where I had my namesake, a young woman called Nirmala who lived with her husband and two children. So I had more help in the kitchen, organised an innovative flower arrangement show in a prestigious gallery. I had to look after welfare activities for the Air Force wives welfare Association as my husband was commanding the unit.

Life was as usual hectic. More than two years were over.

One afternoon I lost my mother due to a sudden cardiac arrest.. We were in the midst of our packing to go on our next posting. The previous week we had the good news that my husband was getting a Vishisht Seva Medal for his meritorious service in the IAF. It was such a pleasant surprise and we called them and told them the happy news. But within a couple of months we heard the sad news that my mother has passed into history. I had to fly to Madras leaving the unpacked steel trunks, boxes and cartons. I had to shake myself literally and leave to see her for the last time. Losing a parent is very painful. Whenever I see her photo my eyes fill with tears.

Once again we moved away from Delhi. It was to Hyderabad.

It is a nice city to live in and my husband's office was in Secunderabad city. Our elder son got through his Entrance exam and got admission in IISc (Indian Institute of Science). He left for Bangalore to join his 4 year course in engineering. Our younger son had to finish his 11 th and 12 th classes in a new Kendriya Vidyalaya. It was good in a way because he could appear for his entrance exams for admission to engineering college in Andhra Pradesh. Everything went on well and at the end of schooling he could join a computer engineering course in Vizag University. But lo behold, we were going to move away from AP to 'Thiruvananthapuram' and our son living in Vizag would have to come to Kerala and that too to the tip of the Peninsula.

I could hardly stay in Hyderabad as I wanted to spend some time with my father in Coimbatore. He was ailing for more than 6 months. I had to be with my son as he was in his twelfth class and had to appear for his final board exams and then entrance tests. Once he joined the engineering college in Vizag I started shunting between Hyderabad and Coimbatore. When my father passed away I started feeling absolutely orphaned and miserable. I felt I had grown terribly old overnight.

But really I was astonished to experience how the ups and downs came in one‘s life.

My husband was to become an ‘air officer’ and was going to take over as a senior officer in charge of maintenance in Southern Air command. We missed my father who would have been delighted with my husband‘s promotion. That sort of joy we can only share with the parents. But nothing stopped. We had to leave for Trivandrum. My husband had to join the new post.

We realised why Kerala is called God’s own country. The natural beauty of the varied landscapes renders the state extremely beautiful. The green expanse of land along the coast was simply breath-taking with mountains, valleys, beaches, backwaters, forests for miles together. Actually we wished we had more time to travel to every nook and corner in Kerala. We did visit the beautiful temples in and around Trivandrum. The temples of Kerala like that of ‘Ananthapadmanabhaswamy’ in Trivandrum and others were built in a different style of architecture, more suitable to the heavy monsoon of Kerala maybe. The wonderful wooden palace at ‘Padmanabhapuram’ is a magnificent edifice in wood. The ancient temple at ‘Suchindram’ and several others were awesome. But the unparalleled beauty, the temple in the tip of India at the confluence of the three mighty oceans, the temple for ‘Kanyakumari’, was strikingly serene and splendid at the same time. It was awesome at sunrise and sunset as well.

My husband had to travel to Andaman and Nicobar islands but I had to stay home all by myself as the boys were away in their hostels. We had no service accommodation in Trivandrum and all were living in reimbursed houses scattered all over the city.

We met quite often at social gatherings and private parties. Ladies club meetings. VIP visits had to be organised and welfare activities had to be planned. I noticed that time and tide never waits whether we like it or not. Days make weeks, weeks become months, months roll on to compose a year.

We had to get ready to perform the wedding of our elder son. As he was leaving to join a university across the Atlantic for his higher studies and the girl he had chosen to get married to, was in the same boat, I mean the same university. Younger son had to travel quite a bit changing trains to come home from Vizag to Trivandrum. He had just one more year left for his graduation and higher studies on alien shores.

Time for my husband‘s retirement was fast approaching too.

Assam Tea Garden

Barracks at Hospital town, Jalahalli, Bangalore.

The Huge Monitor Lizard with whom I was about to share the Bathroom

13

Empty Nesters

We liked our nomadic style of travelling and living in various parts of our country because all four of us went together wherever the posting was and stayed together. In the early years after marriage I did not like the moves much because I had a small baby to look after. As an infant and even as a toddler a baby demands so much attention that a mother can hardly handle a change of place on top of it. To clean, pack and move often especially into temporary quarters of others used to be a huge task. After a few years of such drill I got used to that also and I started liking such a nomadic lifestyle as my children grew up and made life more interesting.

While my husband was committed to his office work the children and I could enjoy the new surroundings, explore and learn more from the friends around us. It is very essential for me as a homemaker to learn about the new place from the school going children as they brought news from their new friends also. We enjoyed going around the new neighbourhood and making friends with people belonging to various regions. It was a huge learning experience.

But all good things also eventually come to an end. It all started perhaps when our elder boy had to fly the nest to join his engineering course in IISC at Bangalore. We were posted in Hyderabad then. Within two years, the younger son had to fly out to Vizag to do his engineering in Andhra University. We moved away to Trivandrum as his father was posted there. So the younger son's Vizag became a faraway place for us, not approachable directly by train. My husband and I missed the boys a lot as we never sent them anywhere away from us till then.

Even as we were getting used to the empty nest syndrome we had to get into yet another change which was my husband's retirement from active service. He had to hang his uniform which he had worn for 33 years. He was just 55 years old. If you compare it to the retirement age in other central government services, which is 58 or 60, it was early. But the thinking then was that the men serving the country's armed forces should be young, maximum in the early fifties or even less. Age, ranks, promotions and scope for promotions depending on age were all closely related. The men serving armed forces had to be young was the general notion those days. Subsequently the retirement age was increased for those serving the military. But by then it did not matter to us as my husband was happily retired and settled too.

In fact my husband was a person who took everything with equanimity, especially things like postings, promotions and retirement. While the boys looked westward to go for higher studies, he looked homeward to decide how to go about settling down in a new home. We were without any help physically or morally as our boys were not there and any little help from the workplace was also not there. Well, it was a retired officers' enclave where we had bought our apartment, but even then getting to do things in a new environment is tough.

When I think back I realise a lot of events happened in the 90s for us. From '87 to '99, we lost both our parents and two of my elder brothers too. It all happened within a matter of a dozen years. We were looking forward to spending a lot of time with our ageing parents without worrying about my husband's annual leave coming to an end or the children's summer vacation coming to an end. We thought our parents could come and stay with us. Alas it was not to be! It was so wonderful earlier when we siblings got together under one roof as the cousins could bond. But all of a sudden the families seemed to shrink. Who shrunk the families? Honey, we did shrink the families. We all became nuclear families because of job requirements. Our children, including those of our siblings too, on finishing their college education, wanted to go away for higher studies and then there was no chance for large family gatherings. Our son got married but he went abroad too along with his young bride.

Anyway we had to look after our future as we had to settle down whether we liked to or not. In our country every little change calls for a lot of work. Take getting a new telephone connection or changing a gas connection. It takes time and a little bit of running around. But things like changing the car registration from state to even just the neighbouring state takes a lot of time. We could not believe we have to pay a lifetime road tax for a car which was on its last leg of life. It was more than 25 years old.

In today's world we would just buy a cell phone and forget about the landline. It was not a digital world back in the 90's. Bulky desk top computers were there, but no transactions were done online. App. Meant an application form, not just one, but three copies to be filled and submitted in an office. App. was not a program available online which could be downloaded to do some task online.

File was one which carried the documents containing a lot of information regarding some work we have done in a government office in the past. For example, take a telephone connection and the papers regarding our connection will be in a file in the BSNL office and if we want to end it and start a new one. We need all the information from that particular file. There will be millions of files in an office. You can imagine how tough it is to locate your file from this huge number of files. Now these data are stored electronically and one can identify a particular file by some reference number. Wow. It seems so easy. But in the 90s we still had documents, bills, papers, or details written down in a fat ledger. So to move them from table to table was a marathon task, considering the ledger was heavy too. We had to pay a heavy price.

Anyway we went about slowly and accomplished our tasks and settled down finally after two or three year's maybe. One thing in a colony is great in which we had our old friends from the days when we were in Air headquarters, New Delhi, Barrackpore, Bangalore, Dinjan, Secondrabad,, & Trivandrum.

We find someone who could guide us and tell us who would help us in that particular area.

14

Y2K, the Year 2000

Y2K, the millennium bug, created quite a stir worldwide in the 1990's. As a homemaker I could not understand much of its repercussions. It was said that western world was particularly worried that a huge disaster might happen when the clock struck 12 o'clock on 31st Dec '99. For some strange reason, I remembered Cinderella's story as to how her fate would change at the stroke of twelve when her carriage with horses would turn into a big fat pumpkin. Oh, sorry, the comparison sounds odious. Well, the shape of our planet is almost the same as a pumpkin, is it not?

We were to enter the 21st century at 12.01am. exactly a minute after midnight on 31st Dec.'99. Will it show 01.01.'? Then....... what? What will happen when the apostrophe before the last two digits stops making any sense? That was the question. It stood for'19' so far from the time computers were invented. The current year followed the '19, like1998, 1999 or whatever. Would it change to 2000 automatically? How? What if the date goes back by a hundred years to 1900? What if it slipped back to 0000? Anything was possible. As usual there were doomsayers who said it was the end of everything; it was 'APOCALYPSE' now.

But let's see how Y2K changed our country. Indians had to study English as our colonisers who ruled us for nearly 300 years made

English the 'lingua Franca'. If ever anyone wanted to study, work and earn a livelihood and be accepted by them, he or she had to know English. Remember 'The sun never set on the British Empire', as the British had started colonising many countries and continents around the globe, sun never set on their empire and along with that on their language too. It became international. Our computer engineers and others, who did computer courses too, had to study English to obtain their degrees, certificates, diplomas or whatever in computer technology. The keyboard and the motherboard of the machine provided their livelihood. Perhaps their understanding of the machine language was better than their proficiency in English language. But in general the world of computers demanded technical know-how, not the rhetoric's of the English language. The computer engineers of our country were sent in droves by our IT giants to the US on H1 visas to carry out a specific project. They went to many countries. Most of them did not expect then that they had to learn one more version of English in the North American continent and even the spellings would change. They had to get through the TOEFL exam of course.

For millions it was the beginning of a new life, not the end of life as predicted. Many countries desperately needed more computer technicians and electronic and electrical engineers. Our qualified young boys and girls got employed in call centres in India. In general they found the millennium bug 'not deadly but friendly', a bug in disguise, dressed in dollars, pounds and rupees too. The outsourced jobs, referred to as Business Process Outsourcing' BPO', were available more easily and jokes about outsourcing were very popular. In short the qualified youngsters had jobs for their asking and our country had thousands of qualified youth who were always asking for jobs.

Ha, ha, but nothing untoward happened at midnight on 31 st.'99. The computers did not go backward or forward by a hundred or thousand years or whatever. The aircrafts continued to fly uninterrupted. The trains were running normally; they did not stop in their tracks at 12 midnight on 31st Dec. '99 not knowing which track to take. The ships sailed. Missiles did not get launched. The power supply did not stop. Water flowed out of the taps. Hey, nothing terrible happened. Thanks to computer whiz kids from all over the world and our whiz kids especially.

Many of the youth who were sent abroad for a specific project happily settled down there, after finishing the project. They found life there more comfortable as the basic facilities were available without any difficulty whether it was gas for cooking or gasoline for the cars. Cars were considered a basic necessity there and they could run them too as fuel was cheap. The roads were so good, at least in big cities in the USA and the roads are better maintained at least in the cities. There were no power cuts and no water scarcity.

Initially the bachelor boys missed their homes, more so during lunch and dinner times, but soon they had their own homes and home loans to worry about. That was that. The single ones got married to girls studying or working there as most of these were love marriages. Some rushed home to get married, these were arranged marriages. For the sake of procuring a visa fast for the spouse they had to do many adjustments as they had to register the wedding first and wait for a traditional wedding for a year or two. I could not follow these rules as they were highly confusing.

By the beginning of the new millennium, many more Indian grocery shops and restaurants came up in every city where the population had a lot of NRIs. Restaurants offered thin dosas, soft idlis, crisp aloo parathas, spicy pickles and chutneys and all of them in fact sold a frozen version of chapatis and cooked vegetables in aluminium foil containers in grocery shops. Many youth had gotten used to surviving on Subway sandwiches, pizzas, tacos, burritos and burgers.

Now in the 21st century perhaps Indian dosas have become as popular and universal as pizzas in any corner of the world. The day is not far off perhaps when dosas would become a regular breakfast item in households across the world.

15

Fashions Change

In our era most of the teenage girls in the south used to wear skirts and half saris, called 'pavadai 'daavani'. As a young girl I had my own ideas of what a 'pavadai 'should be. I wanted it to flow and drape like silk, not stand out stiff and heavy like cotton. Satin or taffeta skirts were good, cheaper than pure silk but satin was too shiny and taffeta was stiff and made a lot of noise while walking. Pure silk was too expensive and could be worn only sparingly. It was for special occasions and festivals only as it could be maintained new for a long time. Naturally it must have been a costly proposition for my father to provide silk skirts for my daily 'wash and wear' use. Hence I preferred to move on to thin cotton sarees for college wear which could be starched, pressed and worn with neat pleats. Now I realise it was some of my teenage whims and fancies to look chic and smart.

Those days the heroines in South Indian movies used to wear pure silk or satin skirts and thin chiffon or georgette half sarees with sequins, beads and embroidery etc... What they wore was not even half a saree; it was just a quarter saree, the size of a dupatta. They looked ten years younger and the outfit camouflaged the bulges and tyres of fat around the waist too. Back then, the film stars were healthy and happy-looking like the rest of the common men and women. Generally people took obesity as the most natural thing to happen in 'middle age'. In other words midriff and middle age coexisted happily.

"Ah, well, we are fat, we are okay with it," actors seemed to say.

"We can act and run around trees singing duets that should suffice," was perhaps what they felt. They were right. They were beautiful with very expressive eyes and nice features and they acted very well. They danced around trees. In short, people enjoyed good food and did not hesitate to take bread, butter and jam along with idlis and dosas on another plate. None had to apologise for looking plump and chubby.

The talented film stars must have believed in working hard but not working out. They ran from studio to studio, not literally, but by cars. Perhaps that was the problem. I am not joking but jogging and walking had not entered the daily routine of young men and women to keep their bodies slim and trim. Perhaps going to the gym was unknown. But today, forget film stars, every woman irrespective of her age wants to have an hourglass figure and look eternally young. Of course people are aware of the health factor but everyone wants to look very young and handsome. Those days I never read about middle-aged film stars and fashionistas in our country stretching the skin on the face, stitching it up, whitening the skin, enhancing and lifting the breasts, getting a nose job done, fixing one inch of eyelashes like 'secretary birds' or eagles, filling the lips to make them look plump and pouting. Many film stars had the teeth and jawline corrected. Today, forget it. Orthodontics every child (who can afford it) gets done, leave alone actors. Teenage girls and boys move around with a mouthful of wires and screws, sacrificing good food in their teens for the sake of good looks and beautiful smiles in their youth.

Come to think of it, we seem to have a lot of problems with the way we look from birth. In short, beauty and looks matter a lot in today's world, rather I can go to the extent of saying looks alone matter.

While in college decades back, we used to discuss the latest fashions sometimes while walking along the corridors in the building. Perhaps we were inspired by a hip-looking girl crossing our path. During lunch break there used to be a lot of girls leisurely loitering around in groups in the college compound. The girls were all avid readers of women's magazines which had pages and pages of models doing the catwalk, wearing various sarees, swimsuits, gowns and other dresses. Miss India, Miss World, and Miss Universe contests were held from 1952 and so we girls loved to see pictures of these beauty contests held in various centres. We were not anywhere close to walking down the ramps or even sitting and watching the pageant. Heroines from Indian movies and Hollywood cinema always attracted a lot of our attention. But that was all we could afford to see. We admired their beauty on the silver screen and printed pages.

Madras was not on top in setting up new trends or even following the fashion scene of Bombay, at least not in the school and college I studied. In Madras many of the parents were still very conservative when it came to dressing. Even girls wearing salwar suits were rare to come by in the south. We only saw saree-clad young, middle aged women wearing sarees and elderly women wearing sarees even in their old traditional styles. In short we saw women wrapped in 6 yards, 8 yards and 9 yards etc. I. Fact it was saree only in south India. Only the length of the sleeves of the blouses and the necklines kept changing from time to time. The vegetable vendors, flower sellers, construction workers and women in the villages used to wear just sarees but no blouses.

Even the sarees were worn by them in a different style, the pleats not coming down to the ankle but just falling below the knees. The pleated pallu was tucked in the waist. Petticoat was absent too. Of course all this was to facilitate them to walk freely. The hot weather was not conducive to wearing blouses indeed. But fashionable women generally opted for sleeveless blouses.

Pure cotton sarees were preferred by many down south as the weather was very warm almost through the year. In fact the whole textiles scenario was changing from the 60's. Our country was famous all over the world for silks and cottons, especially our hand-woven cotton fabrics.

But the synthetics entered from outside, especially from the Middle East, Singapore and Japan. Nylon sarees from these places became extremely popular. The yards of fabrics were said to be used as curtains or stitched up as dresses in other countries, but in our country women wore them as sarees. I must say there were many girls dressed in skirts and half sarees in college but a majority of them wore sarees. Imported 'nylex' sarees were a huge hit. Our own mills produced a lot of synthetic sarees like nylon, rayon, dralon and polyester ones and some silky cotton called 'full voile'. This did not require starching and pressing. Organdie was another popular fabric. This did not require starching at all but pressing was necessary. The synthetic fabrics were used for making salwar, 'kameez' too. They were easily washable, very durable, light on the body and light on the purse too.

After marriage when I crossed Vindhyas I saw the striking difference in fashions. Up north in Delhi women wore mostly salwar, kameez and a dupatta. Dupatta was a part of the ensemble. This was the daily dress of women of Punjab, Haryana, Uttar Pradesh, Jammu and Kashmir and a few more states. The tight fitting churidars were quite popular and the top was kameez or kurta. Kurtas were worn on top of salwar too. Anarkali top, which is a kameez with a lot of gatherings at the waist, was worn in movies by heroines. 'Lehengas' are also the same as full length skirts, which is like 'pavadai' of the south. In most of the states up western part of India, women traditionally wore the ethnic 'lehenga' choli, 'chaniya' choli and. 'Ghagra' choli. The outfit is almost the same though called by different names. It is an ankle length skirt with a lot of gatherings and flair, with a blouse on top worn long or short. But the 'davani' was worn differently. It was called 'odhni'. In Bengal, Odisha, Maharashtra, Coorg, Karnataka and Gujarat to great extent women wore sarees but they were draped very differently in each state.

In the northeast of India, especially in Assam women wore 'Mekhala and chadar' traditionally. This was a two piece outfit but the piece worn at the waist was stitched lengthwise in a straight line. It was mostly 2 yards of raw silk which was wrapped around the waist in a different fashion with a few pleats in Assam. Chadar was a separate upper garment. In Kerala women wore the traditional 'mundu' like lungi and a separate upper garment called 'neriyathu'. This was almost similar to 'mekhela chadar' of Assam.

Up north women, I observed, were very fashion-conscious, and they gave a lot of importance to dressing up. Sarees were meant for formal wear, but daily wear was salwar kameez. Kaftans, nighties and casual pyjama-kurtas were worn as night wear and casual wear. Nighties caught on to the fancy of women all over India. What started as nightwear became 'anytime wear' and many went around even for shopping in nighties to the local shops. It is still very much around.

In the north the women were very particular about colours chosen for summer and winter. The dark coloured sweaters and bright coloured dresses they wore in winter were very different from the pastels for the summer. Wearing sleeveless in summer and full sleeves in winter was the way they chose to dress. Short hair was in and they had their lips painted always at least the armed forces wives were very keen on remaining well-groomed through the day. Eyes were lined and a foundation was applied under the pink face powder from the compact. The chappals were an important accessory. Women in the military were indeed very fashion-conscious. Well, I had to learn a lot when I had to be in their company. The chappals were colourful, embroidered and sequined like those of maharanis. The 'Kolhapuris' were the favourite footwear for many.

Then came the jeans and shirts which started off as the favourite outfit for boys but eventually became so very popular with girls too. Jeans took various 'avatars'. From just looking like a pair of trousers in denim, they became jeans with bell-bottoms, acid-wash jeans, faded jeans, torn jeans, tattered jeans and what-have-you. I have my own children and grandchildren clad in jeans and T-shirts day-in and day-out.

I wonder why boys never showed much interest in changing their fashions drastically. Besides the three piece suit, Safari suit, they have trousers, slacks, jeans, shirts and T-shirts. They wear 'Jodhpuris' and 'Bandhgala' suits on formal occasions of course. Blazers and Tuxedo suits are popular as very elegant formal wear. The men in the southern states and in Maharashtra, Bengal, Bihar, and Madhya Pradesh wear dhotis in different styles. Dhotis worn straight and 'lungis' are the daily casual wear of men down south. 'Sherwani' or silken kurta pyjamas are in vogue now as the wedding dress for young men, North or South the choice seems to be the same, though traditionally the South Indian groom always wore a dhoti with a 'zari' border worn in the cross legged fashion and a matching 'angavastram' to cover the upper body. The 'purohit' would insist that bridegrooms leave the chest uncovered.

Now when I see pictures of heroines from our movies wrapped in sarees I am pleasantly surprised. When they do cat walks on the ramp in sarees, I am amazed. When they say they are proud to appear in a saree on the red carpet in Cannes, I almost faint. But when I look at the picture it is not draped like we ordinary women have been doing for hundreds of years. It is slit, it is stitched, it is split besides being worn in 'seedha' style, Gujarati style, 'Kodava' style, Bengali style, 'Odissi' style, 'Madisar' style and Bharatanatyam style and a dozen other ways. That proves the versatility of sarees. Wow......

In 21st century Indian women prefer to wear gowns and evening dresses for cocktail parties and formal occasions. On the ramp models and fashionistas appear in flowing gowns highly embroidered and embellished with sequins and pearls and precious stones. India boasts of world famous fashion designers and designer garments. The ethnic 'Ghagras' and Chaniya cholis are very popular as wedding outfits even in the south.

Now the most preferred dress for girls and even the older women seems to be salwar suits. Women of all age groups wear salwar suits as daily wear as it is found to be convenient for walking, running to catch a bus, working in the kitchen, working in offices and looking chic and fashionable. The most surprising factor is the seniors are seen moving around in salwar. Across the seas, a stage has come when those who never used to salwar kameez outfit are happily moving around in them. Dupatta is missing from the ensemble. It is there in the movies, as the very flirting between boy and the girl starts with it and is wrapped in it.

Duets in movies as a rule have a dupatta fluttering above the head. But it is on its way out from its original purpose.

"Hawaa mein udtha jaaye, mere Laal dupatta mumulka", as the popular song goes. The dupatta has flown away.

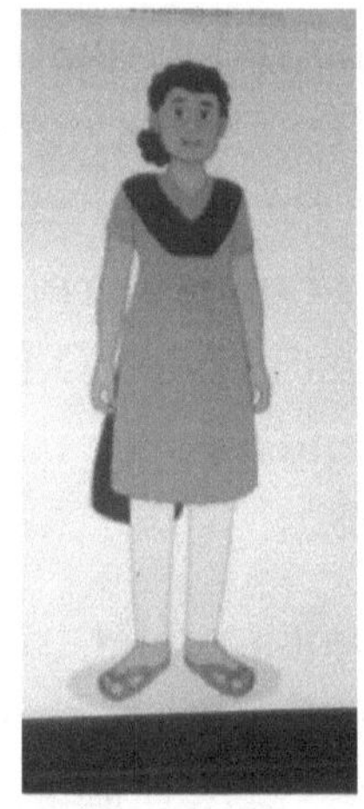

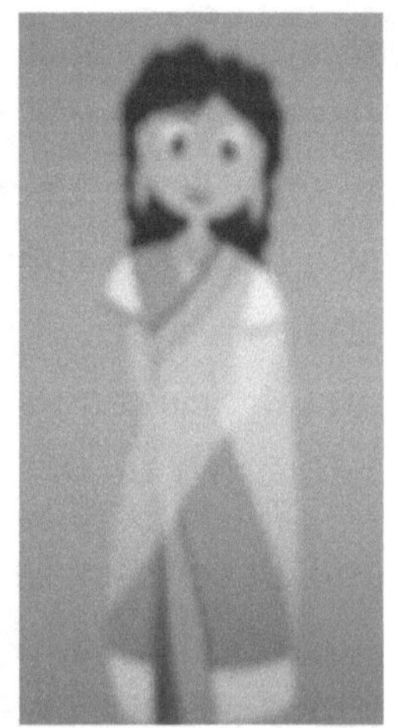

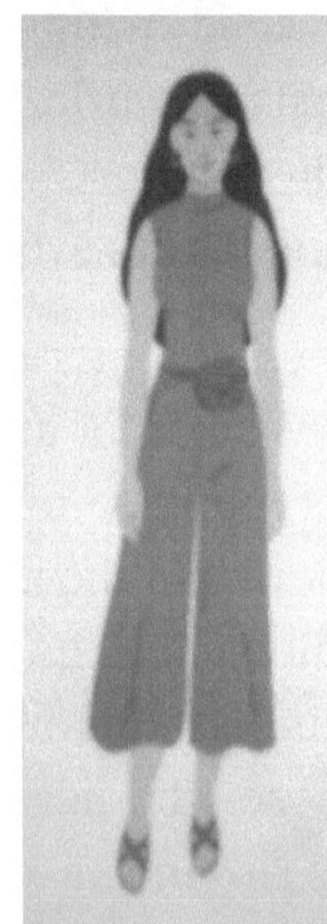

16

Festivals by the Dozens

'Deepavali' is the most favourite festival of all children in India and the most popular festival celebrated in some manner or the other all over the country. As described earlier, just like during summer vacations the children from down the street gathered in my father's house to play outdoor and indoor games, they gathered in front of our gate for firing crackers on Deepavali day.

We used to get up between 2 to3 am as we were excited about this festival of cheer and sheer joy. We went through the ritual of oil bath after my mother applied the warm gingelly oil with pepper corns floating in it on our heads gently rubbing the oil in the hair. And she gave us smooth 'shikakai powder'to wash off the oil. We girls in the family loved the new clothes. So as we finished our bath we would rush to wear the new clothes. I used to wonder why men, even boys, spent time on choosing shirts and trousers. Those days they hardly had four colours to choose from, unlike today when they wear shirts with floral prints and trousers in pink and purple colour and jeans in tatters. They started getting better choices when 'bush shirts,' or 'slacks' were introduced.

Coming back to the early hours on Deepavali day, one by one my brothers' friends dressed in new shorts and shirts would appear with their own packets of crackers outside our gate after their oil bath etc. It was just to fire crackers and have fun together. More the merrier as they say. Those days there was no blanket ban on the sale of crackers due to the pollution it would cause but there were warnings about the dangers it would cause. There were fire accidents reported in the papers of course. We did not hear about anyone falling severely sick the following week. Maybe they did not associate the cases reported to firing of crackers during Deepavali the previous week. I don't know what it was.

Our neighbour, an old man, used to keep a strict vigil and shout at naughty boys every now and then for firing crackers near his windows. That kept the boys under check. Perhaps, the population was less and so the pollution was less. Perhaps the children were not given so much money to buy tons of crackers. Firing 'Lion' brand 'atom bombs' made of jute thread, 'Lakshmi Vedis' rolled in reams of newspaper and 'electric crackers' tied up with string and wrapped in red tissue paper with the image of Red Fort gave the children maximum thrill. Even the simple 'cape', the cute little red dots like today's sticker bindis gave the kids immense joy. We children enjoyed that one day. We were allowed as long as we followed basic precautions. The fun and excitement of watching ground chakra going around or the cute 'tin aeroplanes' take off gave the kids utmost pleasure. These planes went horizontal and hit a pedestrian sometimes; it was then that they were dangerous. Can you imagine a real aeroplane running all over the taxiway and getting into the side bushes instead of taking off into the sky, it was something like that! The tin could scorch the skin. Holding 'Vishnu chakra' in hand, the boys felt as though they were like Lord Sri Krishna holding the 'Sudarshan' chakra. Sometimes it jumped and started rotating loosely but it never beheaded anyone. My father was there to supervise our handling of these crackers. He would ask how we could get so many crackers for

20 or 30 rupees that he gave. The secret was one or two of my elder brothers who were extremely fond of crackers burst their pocket money. One of them was so fond of crackers that wherever he was posted he used to be back home with us for Deepavali. We were really crazy, I think. But we had a blast. You see, we had the other boys with their own supplies too. The whole thing started by 5am or so and went up to 8 or 9am. The morning session was over for us and this was our time for celebration down south.

Then street urchins would appear and pick up unburst 'Olai Vedis', made of dried palm leaves, red 'electric pattas', tiny 'cheena vedis'. These boys, called fire fighters by us, enjoyed making a bonfire of all such unburst crackers. They had their own groups and their own 'dadas' for each group. They were literally street smart and would get into verbal battles and some minor scuffles.

By then we kids were back home and it was breakfast time when we were given all 'bakshanams' on individual plates. In many households idlis and chutney was the usual breakfast on Deepavali morning. The sweets and salty snacks were mostly homemade and anyone at our gate was given some sweets etc. Each Tamil magazine of those days brought out a fat special issue for the festival called 'Deepavali Malar'. There was heavy competition as to who would get to see it first. Of course my father was the first to see and then others got their turns.

'Hey, I get to see that next,' would declare one elder brother.

"No, I only picked it up from that room," another would lay claim." The cover joke on 'Ananda Vikatan' malar by the caricaturist Mali would be repeated by the one who saw it first to everyone else in the family. 'Gopulu' was another hot favourite. His caricatures gave us so much joy. Jokes would be circulating throughout the day. We had our favourite authors of Tamil 'todarkathais' (serial stories) cartoonists and caricaturists. Slowly Kalki, Kalaimagal and Amudasurabhi brought out special 'Deepavali Malars'. My father loved to buy these, voracious reader that he was. Sorry readers, who cannot follow what I am talking about. I was tempted to refer to these which were an essential part of Deepavali for us Madrasis.

. Sweets were exchanged with relatives and friends when they visited or my parents went enquiring 'Gangasnanam acha' instead of asking 'did you bathe in corporation water'? That day's bath was considered as sanctified as bathing in the river Ganges. We had hot water from the copper boiler which we manually mixed with cold water with the help of 'Chombus' (round brass pots) or 'lottas'. There were no plastic mugs those days.

Little wonder our children loved firecrackers as much as we as their parents did. We were shifting from place to place on postings, mostly up north but we had our love for crackers intact which made us buy and enjoy firing them with our kids whenever and wherever we could possibly do. We have lived in apartments on 4 th floor too. Then we could not fire any crackers. The warm oil bath before sunrise was a custom we continued and we bought new clothes of course. When we could have really taken a bath in Ganga or Yamuna water, we could not go around enquiring about our customary 'Ganga snanam acha?' as our friends from the north would not know what we were talking about. Their customs were different. Our boys loved rockets which took off from bottles and the serial electric crackers. A black snake which would roll out from a tablet used to fascinate them. A 'cape gun' every child loved. The whole day they would keep running and shooting.

We exchanged boxes of sweets carefully, remembering not to shuffle and return a box of sweets to the same person who gave it to us in the first place. It happened once when we had more friends dropping in of course. Now we see that the exchange of sweets during 'Diwali' has boosted the sweets and dry fruit sale during the festive season to an unimaginable level. People forget the price rise, inflation etc. as it is a time to burst money too along with crackers.

Firing crackers in the temples during Diwali is gaining popularity all around the world wherever we have our NRI countrymen. We started to light lamps in the evening that was introduced after we started living up north where people celebrate Rama's Return to 'Ayodhya'. We did it happily as we joined the community. Sometimes we had house guests with whom we celebrated as we would in Madras getting up early in the morning. In some stations we gathered in the officers' mess and celebrated. In short Deepavali meant sheer joy. While in the USA we were with grandchildren firing sparklers and flowerpots. There firing Lakshmi vedis and jute bombs were a big no, no. We went to a temple in Chicago to watch their cracker show. It was a beautiful show of 'sparklers showering stars' in the sky drawing multitudes of designs.

Now due to the amount of pollution the tons of fire crackers cause they are completely banned in some places. Some states have restricted timings, which seems a better idea. Some apartment complexes have a common area where they get together and have the Crackers show. Now if India wins a cricket match or if a wedding procession is going on the street, or any festival, they burst crackers for quite a few minutes. The 1000 electric crackers wound up in a string and laid across the street are the most favourite ones for such processions.

We do celebrate Ganesh Pooja, Lakshmi Pooja, Krishna's Janmashtami, Ram Navami, Kartik Purnima lighting lamps, Pongal called Sankranti in Andhra Pradesh and Karnataka and many more Festivals. Some are very ritualistic done inside the homes, some in public pandals, some festivals call for quietly keeping fasts and visiting temples like Shivaratri, and Vaikunta Ekadasi. Our temples celebrate Rath Yatras, Kumbh Melas, and fairs of sorts, which spread the festive spirit all around. I have written more about Diwali and Navarathri because they are celebrated outside homes. They are more of social events like people getting together and celebrating. In short Bharath is an ancient land where people of all religions have lived together for thousands of years celebrating their own festivals in all its splendour.

Another Hindu festival popular in India is Navratri. It is called 'kolu' in the south. It is mainly a women's festival celebrated for nine days and nights. It used to be a back breaking exercise for me as a child as I enjoyed making and arranging dolls on the steps. We girls got dressed up in silk skirts and blouses. Women drew the best of rangolis and arranged the display of dolls using all their creativity and imagination. They made 'sundals' with lentils or made sweets with coconuts, peanuts or sooji etc. Salty snacks like 'murukkus' were made and given to children and women when they came to see the 'kolu' along with betel leaves, 'kum kumam, haldi (turmeric) and coconut etc.

Back in our era, some girls would love to sing the minute they were asked to sing and they would sing the same song in every house. Such repeat performances made the other girls whisper and giggle. The girls would go home with all the bounty and deposit the collection. I am sure their brothers would have made fun of them but they would finish eating everything behind their backs. At the end of their rounds girls would find all their collections missing and minor clashes used to ensue.

Now Navarathri has gone in a different mode altogether. There are competitions sponsored by corporate houses and the TV channels. This has revived the 'kolu' tradition which was losing its popularity in the 80's and 90's. Many people were said to have lost interest in displaying dolls. But thanks to the competition and the attention that the thematic displays attracted, the colourful clay dolls came out of their hibernation. They aired themselves as they came out to stand on the ready-made steps cleaned and repainted too.

Not only in our country but wherever families from south India went, they started displaying 'kolu' in a big way. They even had prizes and a lot of local publicity for the best arrangement. 'Garbha dance during Navarathri, a tradition of Gujaratis, has caught on too and is going worldwide. Dussehra and 'Durga Pooja' is being observed in every corner in India. It is not just Bengalis alone but all other people in the city take part in the festivities. Durga Pooja retains its traditional celebrations from the 'Shashti 'the sixth day to the Dasami, when Durga goes in her victorious procession.

Holi celebrations among North Indians are so popular it has crossed all regional borders. Thanks to Bollywood for that. It has introduced more colour, glamour and romance to the festival. Though it was not celebrated in the south so much when we were children, now we see it has crossed all regional borders. People join any celebration with great cheer.

In general we love holidays and festivals a lot. Halloween, Christmas and Eid festivals spread a lot of goodwill and cheer in our country like elsewhere in the world. We have children in our country going door to door asking for' trick or treat' on 31st October. Carved pumpkins, skeletons, ghosts, serial lights add to the eerie atmosphere. Families display decorated Christmas trees in the living rooms. New Year calls for overnight celebrations from all of us. Friends share 'sevaiya' during Eid. Festivals bring people closer and we love them.

The youth in India celebrate Valentine's Day with more enthusiasm perhaps than Diwali. Mothers and Fathers have special days celebrating them. Earlier it was unheard of. Perhaps the concept of celebrating Mother's Day and Father's Day appeals to our youth more now and they greet their parents. From printed greeting cards they have come to 'WhatsApp' posts!!! In general people love to have fun and that too through cell phones.

The joy of Deepavali - crackers

A tradional Kolu with clay dolls.

The festival of lamps – Karthigai Deepam

Festival of Colours - Holi

17

India Starts Integrating: Do Love Marriages Play a Role?

A major change that transpired as the 21st century dawned was the wedding scene in India. It was a social change which was waiting to happen and it did take place around the turn of the century, perhaps it started in the 80's or 90's itself.

Let me try to explain what I personally feel about the whole issue. Earlier Indians who wanted to enter civil services had to go to London to write the examinations held only there. They came back to serve the Civil services under the British officers holding high posts in the Imperial government. But once the ICS exams were held in India and were open for Indian youth, more of our youngsters could appear and qualify to enter the civil services. From the previous century itself the armed forces, especially the army and the navy, had plenty of Indian personnel serving the Royal Army and Navy. They took part in both the world wars to fight on the side of the British army. The Indian Air Force was established in 1932 CE. Indians were recruited to serve the Royal Air Force. The railways had Indians working at every level from 1853 CE, when trains started running in India. But once the nation became independent in Aug.1947, the floodgates of opportunities opened for our educated men and women, especially for the men.

The ruling came that the Civil Services Examinations, subsequently called UPSC exams, could be written in any of the specified centres in India. Bright young graduates of Indian universities could clear all examinations and interviews in a place of their choice. Depending on the ranks and their preferred options the successful candidates got selected to work in one of the branches of central services like the IAS, IFS, IPS, IRS, IA&AS and perhaps 20 other services for which they qualified. The public sector undertakings were also started in the 50's and they had youngsters coming from all over India to work in them.

The Vindhyas did not divide the nation into two. India was unifying in the real sense of the word. The regional borders started disappearing in the minds of the younger generation at least. It was disturbing to see most of the states were getting divided on linguistic basis. 'Diversity thy name is Bharath', they said but still regional languages played a big role. But many of the citizens were hoping to come closer to each other and belong to the country as a whole.

I think the next generation to ours, who were born in families settled all over India, grew up in more cosmopolitan surroundings. As I said earlier, the children started learning Hindi or any other regional language which they had to perforce learn in school. Now I am coming to the point of my writing as to what I personally think may have happened: within a few years after such integration in the workplace, inter-state marriages started becoming more and more common in our country.

There was a time when down south many marriages were consanguineous especially among people living in Tamilnadu, Andhra Pradesh and Karnataka. The families preferred such alliances inside close family circles. The parents preferred to give their daughters in marriage to uncles and first cousins. Farthest they would go to a second cousin or marriage to someone already well known to the family circles. Arranged marriages were almost the order of the day. Even now they are the rule in many families in our country but there are more exceptions to this rule all around.

From strict arranged marriages it slowly came to marriage alliances by love 'happening' between the boy and the girl from two different communities, castes, regions, religions and races. In short, love marriages may not have become an everyday affair but not an affair to raise an eyebrow or raise a hue and cry about. We were nearing the dawn of a new millennium when this started happening more.

As a result the traditional and highly conventional wedding celebrations which differed from region to region and even from family to family changed further. The parents had to accept a mixing of traditions from the rest of India and even the rest of the world.

For instance, our (Telugu-speaking) son decided to get married to a girl coming from a Tamilian family.

The first question which struck me, a mother from a conservative family, was how the 'Mangal sutra' was going to be designed. They follow basically different designs. Was it going to be called 'Bottu' In Telugu or Thali in Tamil? How about the saree which the bride will wear at the time of 'mangalyadharanam' tying the 'thali'. Was it the 8 yards of yellow cotton saree with a little zari in the Telugu fashion or 9 yards of red silk saree worn in 'madisaar' style (cross legged) or 6 yds. Saree to be worn in plain Indian style? Actually we were amazed by the different customs we followed in the rituals and how we stuck to them!

'How about the priest, is he going to be Tamilian or Telugu?' was the next question cropping up. Ultimately the bride's father brought a Tamil priest from Maharashtra and we got our Telugu priest from Tamilnadu. The integration went to another level. The priests perhaps had to discuss and choose the rituals as per their desire.

Finally it was a happy fusion of customs mutually agreed. 'Oonjal' (swing) was one such custom, not our family tradition, but we agreed to have it. 'Oonjal' songs were sung by a group of ladies led by my sister. It was a colourful tradition accompanied by singing and swinging. The ladies swung into action, taking aartis with coloured rice balls and lamps made of rice flour and throwing them in all directions to take off the effect of any evil eye falling on them. Everyone enjoyed it including the bride and groom.

The 'seer bakshanams' (sweetmeats) consisting of salty snacks like 'murukkus' in concentric circles and laddus in various shapes from the round balls to conical structures were ordered from a sweet shop. Making sweets and salties to give the 'sammandhis' used to be a major 5 day project in South Indian weddings. They were made at home in hundreds and stored. A pair of 'paruppu thengai' was the typical sweets made for any auspicious function in the south and they stood towering above other sweets like temple towers in a village. Perhaps compared to getting the 'bakshanams' (snacks)made at home which required space to keep the stove to cook and fry, supply of essential ingredients, space and containers to store the sweets and saving them from ants and kids etc., this outsourcing was found to be so very convenient. Yes, the kids had a field day when they were made at home. But the packed sweets arrived straight at the venue on the day of the wedding. Naturally the kids were denied the joy of tasting them days before the wedding. But it could not be helped.

As my siblings and I reached middle age our nephews and nieces started getting married. The wedding was inter-state again. One nephew's wedding was in Bombay as the girl's parents lived there. The rituals followed were a happy mix of those from Maharashtra, Karnataka, Tamil Nadu and Andhra Pradesh as the boy was Telugu and the girl was Kannada + Marathi mix. There was Sathyanarayana Pooja, Sangeet and mehndi on Day 1. Mehndi we applied in our families earlier but it was not a huge function. It was a messy affair, mehndi applied with fingers, not icing cones. We did not have intricate and complicated designs running up to elbows etc. Down south we sang classical songs while Aartis were taken, no singing of film songs by groups of ladies. The latter is fun of course and the girls prefer it..

On Day 2 the 'mangalsutra' was tied. The bride had worn saree Kannadiga style, the headgear worn by the bridal couple was Maharashtrian, and there was a beautifully decorated set of 'kalasams' in the mandap which was a special feature of Marathi weddings. It was a beautiful mix and match. The reception in the evening had the special dishes of Bombay, Bangalore and Madras being served hot in the food stalls.

On day 3 was the grand finale, a cocktail party. Champagne bubbling in tall tulip glasses was served to the assembled guests. Dance by the couples gave the celebration a gala finish. Is it not the way to go? East met west. The fusion was complete. Everyone enjoyed the evening.

Then came the other nephew's wedding. He married a Telugu girl whose parents lived in Gujarat and the girl, a doctor, had lived in Gujarat all her life took part in the garbha dance along with her cousins, friends and most women in the crowd. It was beautiful to watch the hands covered in henna designs gracefully going up and down clicking the sticks going around the lamp. Most of them including the young bride were dressed in bright flowing ghagras embellished with sequins and pearls. It was grand and glamorous, like a scene out of a Bollywood movie. 'Deepam' (a lamp) was there, but Deepika was not there. That was new to us going from Madras. The next morning, the religious rituals were typically Telugu. The groom's party enjoyed two days of exotic food from all corners of India from dhokla to dosas. It turned out to be a 'midsummer night's dream dinner'. The reception was in the middle of June under the starry sky.

We had the wonderful experience of getting our younger son married in a Venkateswara temple in Chicago, USA. He was getting married to a pretty Telugu girl who had her schooling, graduating in a law college in Pune and post-graduating in Chicago. The sastrigal was there, performing all the religious rituals as per our Telugu traditions of Kashi Yatra, Kanyadanam and Mangalya dharanam. But in Andhra tradition it was the cumin jaggery paste being applied on the bride's head by the boy and the same mix the bride keeping on the groom's head was considered the most significant ritual. It was symbolic that the couple should be inseparable and stuck to each other like jaggery and cumin forever.

Come to think of it, our weddings have a lot of symbolic rituals like tying mangalsutra, exchanging rings, garlands, applying 'sindoor' on the bride's parting in the hair, the baraat, the 'saath phere', and a lot more. You can write a book on it.

But the sastrigal in Chicago had to see that place was not too messed up with turmeric powder or the "cumin jiggery" paste. It had to be applied with great care. Havan (homam) had to be restricted to an AL foil container with burning charcoal. There could not be much fire without smoke but at the same time the fire had to be there as a witness to the wedding without creating too much smoke. As smoke could set off the alarm, there was the chance of fire brigade descending on the scene and none wanted them to disrupt the rituals. But nothing happened. The purohita (sastrigal) had performed hundreds of Hindu weddings and that too in temples. He knew how to go about the whole ritual beautifully.

The temple arranged for a nice feast after the wedding proper. Year after year, lots of weddings are performed in various temples in the USA. The NRIs have their local friends come and enjoy watching the Hindu ritualistic celebrations. We had our close family members and friends attending the wedding too.

There have been so many integrated weddings in our own family circles that I can go on and on. The borders started disappearing between states. We kept getting news from our own circle of relatives and friends more often. A Tamilian boy tied the knot with a Punjabi girl. Karnataka groom wedded a UP girl. A Telugu girl married a Bengali boy. Yet another girl got into a marriage alliance with a Kashmiri bridegroom. If the couple decide to tie the knot or sign a register or just cross a threshold of their own house or whatever, the rest of customs and whatnots did not seem to matter anymore. Even living together before getting married has caught the fancy of boys and girls. We have seen many a white boys marrying Indian girls and white girls married to Indian boys according to Vedic traditions and recitation of mantras. In fact the white brides or grooms are very keen on learning the meaning of the mantras too.

When the world is becoming flat everything will be a happy mix as the famous writer says it is a "level playing field" perhaps for boys and girls to choose with whom they would team with in professional lives as well as whom they team with in their personal lives.

The latest trend seems to be couples picking whatever custom they fancy, whatever ritual they like irrespective of where it is from. It is left to the choice of the couple to pick and choose the venue. It could be a palace in Rajasthan if they can afford it or a simple wedding celebration with just the family members in a temple. The couple discuss and decide the guest list and the menu for the feast. The invites are designed and dispatched personally by the couple themselves. The parents just give support whether physical, moral or financial or whatever. The designer 'lehengas' are bought not only for the bride but for her whole family and close friends too if they too want to wear designer lehengas or sarees. Today the expenses can run into not just lakhs but crores.

Traditions are changing. For ages the bride in the south used to be dressed in a dazzling tissue saree of Kanchipuram woven with zari threads with very little silk ones interspersed or a 'oosivanam saree which was woven with more silk threads and lesser zari threads. A few preferred Banarasi brocade weighing heavy with intricately woven border and pallu. Now it is lehengas for the reception and there are more guests only for the reception. I am sure the tissues will eventually return to the wedding scene. After all, fashions go in circles.

Anything is fine, I presume, as long as the couple decide to live happily ever after, or rather stick to each other like cumin and jaggery paste.

Integrated wedding of to-day.

Mehndi

18

Our Herald Triumphs

The days of rolling up my infant son in a blanket and having him cling to my chest and riding pillion in a Lambretta scooter from Rajokri, (New Delhi) to anywhere and everywhere in Delhi came to an end at last. My husband decided to buy a car, bought one for which he went all the way to Madras by train and drove it back by road, risking driving through Chambal valley, to Delhi. Incidentally he could check how the second hand car (in his eyes it looked brand new) behaved in the 'long run' literally. Actually it did have the longest run any car could have had with a single owner, the previous owner had it for less than a year perhaps. By the way the owner was a lady.

At last we had the freedom to move around the capital without getting anxious and tense about the trips by two wheeler. More than us, every one of our relatives we visited in Delhi got worried when we got down from the scooter.

"In this biting cold weather you came by scooter. Oh, god, come sit next to the room heater. Such a tiny baby he is," my aunt would chide me and take the baby from me.

Obviously they were genuinely concerned as the distance was quite a bit and they knew I could not have held onto anything in the scooter. But once we got our car we started going out more often as our guests wanted to go visit our relatives and go sightseeing too. They were taken to watch 'Son et Lumiere' in Red Fort and a walk along Chandni Chowk, with a stopover at 'Ghantewala' sweet shop to buy 'Sohan halwa". We drove to 'Rajghat' to pay our respects to the father of the nation. Jan path, Connaught Place and Karol Bagh were a must for shopping, especially for buying cane baskets, 'modas', handbags, purses, kaftans and colourful 'chappals'. We too enjoyed the trips as we were exploring Delhi along with them.

Two of my classmates from school shifted to Delhi as their husbands were transferred to Delhi. One more couple, close friends of ours were my friend's elder sister and her husband. We visited these three houses very often. Our spouses became friends and our sons became friends. Literally when we met the whole family had fun. We had multiple choices in that we could go to one friend in Green Park or another in Railway Colony near 'Chanakyapuri' or yet another in New Friends colony. We lived in R.K. Puram. Those days not many had a television at home. Two of them bought a TV set earlier than us. That was their mistake. It was a great treat for us as it turned out to be a two-in-one deal for us, a meal and a movie. These days remain unforgettable as we were all young at that time. For all these trips we had our Triumph Herald.

While in Delhi we drove our car to Haridwar, Rishikesh and Lakshman Jhoola, Mussorie, Dehradun, with my parents-in-law. The best was all of a sudden we were tempted to go up to 'Badrinath' in our car with a "supercharger' at the wheel, who happened to be my husband. When my husband asked one man standing guard where the road started climbing up for Badri, he took one sad look at our car and declared: "sahib, nahin, "aap is car mein nahi jaa sakte hain".

(Sir, no, you cannot go in this car) He shook his head very sadly but repeatedly. He glanced inside the car in which he found three generations of people, a grandfather, father and son. We took a 'U turn' and started our journey back to Delhi.

But as I had written earlier, we settled in Delhi nicely. It was January '71. Just then the Bangladesh war was over. I had come with my mother back to Delhi along with my elder boy and an infant son. Our car took us on various visits to the child specialist and on our regular search for procuring tins of baby food. Those days there was a severe scarcity of tinned baby food. This 'battle for baby's bottle food' had to be fought by my husband all by himself. For the other war with the neighbouring nation to liberate Bangladesh, he had the entire armed forces with him.

Anyway we had to move out of Delhi after spending half a dozen years in two postings. We were moving closer to Bangladesh. Our car came with us wherever we went on posting whether it was by road, by train or by air. It almost became a member of our family. This time the trip to Calcutta for our 'herald' car was by train.

The car manufactured in '66, was just a year older than my son. We learnt to move around the new city Calcutta in our car. Those days, except for the pedestrians, there was no help or guidance from google maps or any other map in new cities for the drivers to drive around. But mostly people we asked for directions were helpful. Our little son joined a new school. We could get some good domestic help and sort of settled down. But lo behold, the posting came. Our stay in 'Barrackpore', Calcutta was less than two years even.

My husband was required to undergo a 6 month refresher course at his Alma mater, the Air Force Technical College in Bangalore. Our new found Bengali friend in Calcutta planned for a sightseeing trip in Odisha along with us by our cute little car. He wanted to enjoy a holiday with us before our departure from Calcutta. We liked the idea too as we had not seen Odisha.

Readers, can you imagine how the two-door Standard Herald car would have been with 4 adults and 4 children. It was jam packed. Thankfully it had only two doors on the whole. If there were back doors and they were opened accidentally a little boy or girl might have fallen out. That 'tight', the packing was in the back seat. We were young alright but, hey, we required space to sit. The kids were small alright but they needed leg space at least if not b..m space as our laps provided that. But we could take it all laughing and joking. We were busy sightseeing. Our first major stop was at the capital of Odisha, Bhubaneswar (leaving the p-breaks in between, the trees and bushes by the side of the roads became the rest rooms on the highways). We stayed two days there. After that we went to 'Puri' for two days. The next stop was 'Konark' and there our friend's family took leave of us. From there they had to go back to Calcutta.

Our journey continued. We passed through a heatwave in Andhra Pradesh in our non-air-conditioned car. I have described it in an earlier chapter. We reached our destination Madras, a week after we left Calcutta. My husband as usual patted the car fondly and thanked it too. He spoke to it like people speak to their pets and plants.

After a tour of the east, we went down to Kanyakumari the very next week along with my in-laws and my husband's siblings. My husband liked such cross country trips a lot then. We saw quite a few temples down south like Tiruchendur, Udupi, Dharmasthala and Kollur etc. My parent's in-law loved the trip to temples a lot. What made them happier was the fact that their son took them on the pilgrimage in his own car.

After all the tours we reached Bangalore right on time for the course, of course. The little darling 'Herald triumph', triumphantly went from Calcutta to Cape Comorin like a loyal friend never letting us suffer. Remember, it was not air conditioned, hey, it did not even have 4 doors to boast of, but it ran. Even when the outside temperature was 45 degree C in Andhra Pradesh while he was driving through from Calcutta to Madras, our 'Herald' remained cool and ran without getting into heated arguments. He might have fretted and fumed a bit. But he did not feel exhausted.

We were very familiar with Bangalore as we both had seen it many times. But earlier my husband did not have a car when he joined the Air Force Technical College for the ''ab initio' course for training to join IAF.

Any new place we went my husband would locate a car mechanic first even before looking for a good paediatrician for our children. We had a great time in the city as we had a lot of family functions to attend. We attended weddings of siblings and cousins. We celebrated a number of festivals together with families on both sides. Weekends were spent in Salem with my in-laws. Our Herald did those trips. Holiday trips to Madras were by train mostly. The car took us many times to Mysore, Nandi Hills and other tourist spots in and around Bangalore with guests too.

From Bengaluru we moved to Assam. Now the car came in a container van by train. Poor thing was chained like a slave to the sides of the carriage and he arrived intact without moving this side or that side. But his heroic performance was yet to come. By then he had spent a dozen years with us. He already showed signs of ageing. He was only entering his teens. One problem was his slow running jet, whatever it meant, would conk off whenever he was slowed down. We were living in the midst of a jungle in 'Dinjan'. Close to our house was the taxiway the British had made for their planes to land and take off during World War II. It had remained unused for thirty five years. Eventually it became the habitat of leopards, black panthers, foxes, iguanas, monitor lizards and snakes of sorts.

One evening around 6 pm. we were returning home from some grocery shopping.

"Shall we go inside the taxiway to try our luck today", asked my Husband casually.

"Yes, yes, let's go," the boys said in one voice enthusiastically. My parents-in-law were in the back seat along with the boys. The boys were so eager to see panthers and leopards in the wild. We had tried a couple of times earlier without luck. It was the practice in that Air Force unit that whenever any person came across a family of leopards or a single one roaming around they, would report it to the air force personnel. That night a cage would be set up in that particular location with a goat as bait. The poor goat would keep bleating and this was a give-away for the predator as it would walk towards the cage. But as it would enter through the open end instantaneously two shutters would fall, one behind the predator and the other between the prey and the wild beast. The goat would bleat pitiably and the beast would roar. But anyway the goat would be alive next morning. In fact the goat was named 'Miss Dinjan' as she set a record of catching eight leopards.

So till then we had only seen the spotted leopard cubs caught in the cage.

But that evening we innocently drove deep inside the narrow single track with thick bushes on both sides. The growth became denser. The taxiway had been deserted and forsaken for decades together while panthers and leopards made it their home. And all of a sudden our 10 year old boy who was sitting in between his grandparents perhaps could spot a pair of glassy eyes staring at us from a distance. He said excitedly, "oh, they are there. Today we have caught them,". The 6 year old joined, "oh, yes, yes, they are there," It was pitch dark and the panther was jet black but its eyes shone when the headlights were shining on it. It did nothing. No movement. We all could see four cubs all around the mother. There she was a huge black panther lying down on a narrow pathway in front of our car at a distance of about 50 to 60 yards. Slowly the mother stood up with its tail erect, perhaps ready to strike. We had heard others describe such postures and accidental sightings.

We were awe-struck, speechless almost. We could not scream. We could not honk the horn. My husband had to slow down the car and if it stopped, the engine might conk out, in which case the car had to be pushed from the back by who else, but our little boys. Oh, no. My husband was crawling very slowly if he went closer and if the mother-leopard came near the car, she could just lift her front legs, peep in and hit the window with her powerful paws. Six of us in all age groups would have been sitting ducks for the mother and her four cubs. Thankfully the Dinjan panthers were not man-eaters like tigers of 'Kumaon'. Oh, God, I could hear our heartbeats in our ears.

When we were about 15 yards from her, the mother started crossing the road with two of her cubs following her and the other two perhaps went deeper into the bushes on the other side. My husband drove ahead slowly first without looking this way or that way till we crossed her and our boys were looking from the windscreen at the back to see that the panther cubs were safe. The car roared a couple of times and then picked up speed. We went so fast. I think my husband had never driven it faster than that night, never ever. The eyes of the panther were scary indeed. They glistened like a couple of powerful torch lights in the darkness. Had our car stopped inside the jungle none would have known till the next morning perhaps as none knew we were in the jungle.

Those thrilling moments passed. From Assam we went to Delhi and then down to Hyderabad and Trivandrum we had to go on postings. Herald flew in the underbelly of an aircraft not once but twice.

In pouring rain we went with our NRI guests from Trivandrum to Kanyakumari. It was a non-stop downpour. Our friends, both were good drivers and they owned some of the top end cars. The husband asked my husband, "You think it is okay to drive. Maybe we can stay here "overnight," He sounded so worried. It was around 7pm. He was sitting on the edge of the seat and could not take his eyes off the road. The wiper went 'tick, tick, tick, tick, it kept wiping the windscreen continuously and the rain was incessant.

My husband told him very confidently, "don't worry; I will take you both home safely. I have driven in worse conditions,"

But our Herald was our friend. He didn't betray us. We reached home safely. The inanimate tiny low–slung car had decided to be with us, come rain or sunshine. Perhaps he handled the rains better than a bigger car ever could.

Readers, that car stayed with us for 25 years like a faithful dog, on the whole it celebrated its silver jubilee with us, and 25 years is a long period. It did bark at times when the engine had starting problems. It was push-started many times. We never left home without the tools and some four transmission bolts and nuts. It had an external horn. On one occasion it had an external petrol tank briefly.

My husband simply loved the car. He used to pat it and run his fingers on the bonnet lovingly quite often just like dog lovers run their fingers tenderly through the fleece on the backs of their pets. We had tears when we parted with it one day. We told the mechanic who bought the car to keep it. He said he was going to rent it out for wedding processions. But, no, after a few months my husband heard that the car was broken and sold as scrap. That was the tragic end for old cars. We both were shaken. We loved him a lot. Who says cars don't have feelings. Our Herald had a heart of steel no doubt, but strong like gold and soft as silver.

Our Herald Triumphs.

19

Grandchildren Beckoned

We started travelling across the Atlantic once our children went for higher studies and then decided they would work for a few years there and come back. We are still waiting for the 'come back' of course.

Well, when the first grandchild was due to arrive we made our first trip. We were absolutely thrilled about becoming grandparents. It was but natural for us to feel we should help them a little initially as with a new-born the workload increases exponentially and the chores become endless. As parents they may be finding the new situation very new, puzzling and demanding. I thought they would need some advice and help from us.

I remembered how my mother used to attend to my little son's demands intuitively with great expertise. She used to handle the baby's colic pains at 2am night after night. She will sit with the baby asking me to sleep. She used to give oil baths to a tiny bundle of joy, slippery and soft, who would constantly try to wriggle out from her firm grip. She would squat on the floor of the bathroom, hold the oily infant on her outstretched legs, massage him with oil and then bathe him with the special home-made powder. She did it with great confidence.

I just stood and watched in awe or poured water on him with great care. I was least prepared for anything that was in store for me including the extreme intensity of the labour pain. I read some books perhaps on child care but nothing I ever discussed with my mother or with my OB-GYN about my pains, birthing, breathing or how to handle the new-born. These things were sort of taken for granted that when the time came we would learn somehow, but how? But I did not know how I would cope. We were not very open about certain topics. My husband and I did not attend any Lamaze class to prepare us as to how to handle the situations, from pregnancy to childbirth and looking after a new-born, which we were going to face.

But you see, we had the easiest way out. I had to just board a flight at New Delhi and reach my parents' home in Madras within a few hours. The rest of the 'works and services' my parents, especially my mother would take care of. My mother had the same luxury of going to her parents' home to deliver all her six kids. In her case her parents and grandma looked after her. I knew that I was born at home in the middle of the night with the help of a midwife. My grandparents, my great grandmother and a couple of helpful aunts looked after me and the rest of my elder siblings too. My mother was lucky indeed!!!

Well, coming to my daughter-in-law, who was going to deliver her first baby, a would-be-natural citizen of the USA living in Pittsburgh, USA. We thought we had to be by our daughter-in-law's side as a moral support to help her in whatever way we can. I thought like my mother, my sister and aunt etc, who came with me to the nursing home when I got admitted for delivery, I would be going with my daughter-in-law and sit outside in the corridor. But no, I was not supposed to go. In the USA the entire procedure was different. We could not crowd around like we do here.

For one patient at least five attendants will be there, and visitors any number.

The couple were all set physically and mentally to manage the situation. In my case when I was in labour pain my husband was in Delhi and I was in Madras. But in my daughter-in-law's case, her husband was there at home with her to count the contractions and then take her to the hospital at the nick of the moment and admit her. He was still counting the frequency of the contractions and then got himself admitted inside the room to receive the not-so-clean baby, cut the umbilical cord and bond with the baby and make the sticky baby bond with the mother, a sort of set procedure. He was required to be with her throughout. I was amazed. How different the whole scene was!

So, my husband and I had to stay at home and patiently wait for our son's phone call. First the call came and then my son came and took us both to see the new-born granddaughter. I was told that she delivered in the same room which looked very much like the ward to which I came hours after delivering my baby except that the one in the USA was much bigger.

In my era I was inside the theatre with just my doctor and nurses while my mother, my aunt and sister were seated on the chairs outside in the corridor. They must have been waiting with bated breath to find out about my latest delivery-status. I must have been screaming and struggling alone on the table or whatever. Suddenly I must have become quiet as I was sedated. They got worried. It seems my mother and the rest were looking at the door of the theatre to see whether the nurse walked out to give the latest bulletin about the delivery status. At last they were relieved to hear about the safe arrival of the baby hours later. I had delivered a baby boy. They were thrilled to hold the baby when the nurse let them touch him hours later after he was bathed and cleaned.

The grandparents living in India and their NRI grandchildren born on alien shores are worlds apart. The whole scenario is different. My husband and I went every time a new grandchild was born. We helped with looking after the new-born and feeding the parents of course. We played with the baby a lot. The babies grew up in basins, tubs, cribs, bouncers, car seats and strollers. The pacifiers seemed to be the easiest way to pacify them. The children born there grew up in the culture of the adopted country. But the time grandmothers like me spent with them as infants and mischievous toddlers remain etched in our memories. We fussed, cuddled, kissed, spoke and even sang to the baby.

Engrossed in watching TV

20

Time for Grandparents to Regale

When the children became two years old or even less they wanted stories whether it was from their story books or from our own collection of 'grandma's tales'. At this juncture I would like to say Panchatantra Kathas and Amar Chitra Kathas helped us to bond beautifully with the children. Our epics Ramayana and Mahabharata were eternal source of favourite stories for both the narrator and the listeners. Kids loved Jataka tales and Vikramaditya stories found in 'Vetala Panchavimsati'.

But as the children grew up, they wanted some new story everyday if possible. My husband and I used to tell them stories of our own childhood even. We watched 'kid' movies, I mean Disney movies.

Fairy princesses were one girl's favourite. She moved around with a tiara and a magic wand. We saw Kung Fu Panda at least 50 times and 'Despicable me' with minions a million times. Jungle book every day once for 1 month because our granddaughter loved it. We made a Jurassic park in the nursery of our grandson. We did whatever they fancied like drinking imaginary tea in tiny cups and saucers. As a grandma I was changing dresses for Barbie dolls and combing her silky blond hair whatever little was left uncut by the granddaughters. The girls were the hairdressers for their Barbie dolls. They would knot them and curl them as they liked till their mothers stepped into their room and caught them scissor-handed. I feel they were itching to do this perhaps as they had undergone the hair cutting sessions at the hands of their mothers.

Grandpa gave rides on his back to the kids. One child liked playing with Lego blocks and the other would insist we do a 1000-piece-jigsaw puzzle (an equally tough and back-breaking exercise) with her. Yet another teased us with a battery-operated T-Rex pouncing on us or biting us. My grandson told me birds were the only species left which descended from dinosaurs. He was an Encyclopaedia on 'Dinosaurs and Birds'. One would tell me stories of science fiction movies. It was fun all the way. I never thought one day I would be learning from my grandkids how the earth came to be billions of years ago, I think it was 4 billion(not sure) with a 'BIG BANG'. They asked a million questions when I told them our view of creation. I did not create unnecessary confusion in their minds about our theory of creation and what they were taught in school about the theory of evolution. I generally agreed with them that their theory of evolution was right.

Those were such wonderful years as they made us feel young again. In the board games that we played with them we had to lose. Whether it was 'Uno' or 'a game of donkey," with playing cards or 'Bingo', the grandparents have to lose. That was an unwritten rule as the joy of winning had to be theirs. When these kids grew up and started going to elementary classes we walked with them to their schools if the school was close by. If they went by car we went with our daughters in-law to pick them up or drop them at school.

Come to think of it, with our own children we did not spend that much quality time. We mothers were in the kitchen most of the time or at the dining table either feeding them or doing homework with them. But when the grandchildren came along we were free to spend more time with them as the major responsibility of running a house, shopping for groceries, cooking etc. was not our job. Our daughters-in-law did the tough job.

Travelling with grandkids was a pleasure, listening to their favourite songs, we seniors felt refreshed. The songs were from Bollywood movies, 'Indie pop', Jennifer LO, Michael Jackson or Abba and just anything and everything they fancied. We played. 'Word games' or 'stone, scissors, paper' game. 'I spy' game with things we saw around us used to be so interesting. We have several of our own indigenous games like 'ammakuthu', 'dimmakuttu', 'Pattikuthu'......'trying to arrest the toddler's 'tiny fists' in ours with our two open hands. Even "kottaprandu kannukutha varudu, varudu...." to scare or tickle the 8 month old with our index and middle fingers acting like pincers used to keep them amused. The toddlers seated in their car seats enjoyed such games immensely. They would get tickled even without us touching them. Such joyful giggles with a toothless mouth were a picture of pure innocence and sheer delight.

We travelled quite a bit by car. Hours flew by and when we reached our tourist destination the parents and children would happily eat veggie burgers, French Fries or some layered sandwiches. But we seniors were really not very fond of such hard stuff. My problem was I did not have a mouth so wide and a healthy set of teeth to bite.

But after a long drive walking through geo wonders like geysers, stunning canyons, arches, bears and wild buffaloes in national parks, we would feel ravenously hungry. We were picky about food and wanted to avoid many ingredients like cheese, sugar, strange spices, garlic, mushrooms or whatever, depending on our systemic problems. Sightseeing, we expect to get 'idly' or 'dosa' with a chutney and Sambar. Actually we were surprised when our son could get frozen lemon rice, Palak paneer and a couple of rotis even, when we were in the midst of three northwest states of the US like Montana, Wyoming and Idaho. They look so vast, rocky, and barren with wild buffalos and bears moving around and we expected spicy and tasty Indian food without garlic and mushrooms. There was a time ages back my eldest brother used to say if a vegetarian wanted to travel in Europe or the USA, he or she should be ready to manage with bread, biscuits, buns, fruits, nuts and salads. But in today's world, especially in the USA, a lot of their cities have restaurants serving typical Indian food and grocery shops stocking frozen Indian food. Wow. Incredible!!!

But our grandchildren have grown up eating this day in and day out and they love them. They see their friends bringing them in their lunch boxes. They get influenced by other children too. If only we learn how to enjoy life along with them, we can live our second childhood without care. There are many ways to bond with children. Even enjoying what they like is one of them. I try to tell myself that they imitate the adults in their actions and reactions, likes and dislikes too. When they enter teens they have their own friends and phone calls. They get loads of complicated projects where they have to make a helicopter or a drone which can actually fly.

They have no time to breathe when they go to high school. So it is best to enjoy before they enter their teens and become 'freshmen' or 'sophomore'. It's okay for us to say 9th or 10th class too.

I played with barbies while grandpa sat with Lego blocks

21

None Asks for My Opinion

21st. Century started surging ahead. There I was living with my husband in our house at the end of the road in a cul-de- sac opposite a beautiful mango grove on the banks of the Adyar river (8 to 9 months in a year, the river does not flow, it remains stagnant, slushy and yucky). I had a popular magazine in my hands going through the opinion polls done on nuclear families and joint families. I would have loved to take part in such discussions, but no one ever asked me. Who are these lucky people who give their opinion and it is in print?

I have never seen anyone come to our house, I mean youngsters who conduct opinion polls. Agreed, it is the last lonely house close to a park. There might be snakes slithering by in the park nearby, maybe cobras, but they don't bite unless you step on them. The roads were safe as we very rarely saw a snake slithering by. One odd day you may see an exciting fight between a snake and a mongoose. Yes, I agree en-route on the road people might have to face stray dogs, but again they might bark, but not bite, (hm.... I go purely by the saying 'barking dogs do not bite'). Sometimes street lights would be off and in monsoon our road, which ends in potholes and muddy patches, might be slushy, then it could be awful. But anyway opinion polls are done in daylight, not in the night.

All those young people who walked around with bulky backpacks holding sheets of papers, ready to evangelize, debate, convince, request, and listen to your viewpoint, about any topic of public interest, never asked me for my opinion. Never, ever. I have so much to say and yet no one asks me for my valuable input. Forget about me, they have not asked my siblings, uncles, even second and third cousins, or friends living in any location in the city. Yet they publish those mysterious polling results on any topic about hospitals, schools, universities, living-in relationships, love marriages, raising children, single parenting, taking care of old parents or pets or anything under the sun.

After all, I have lived long enough, seen the world pass through several 'yugas' almost. I have heard news and views from the ancient 'word of mouth' to the latest, 'WhatsApp' posts zooming across continents in a matter of split seconds. In fact, my family feels I have an opinion on everything from the T-shirts my children wear to how to run a certain system or institution better. What is the use?

Many a time auto drivers, taxi drivers, and some private car owners would think this alley was a short cut to the main road on the other side of the colony, but they would see the road come to a dead-end. When they see the huge black Iron Gate and a black board announcing the end of the colony they would get very angry. Using the worst cuss words in two or three languages, they take a rash turn and zoom off in a great rage desperately trying to catch the 'precious' three minutes that they lost in this manoeuvre.

Sorry for digressing but I wish someone would do a poll on men using impolite language in public. How often we old timers are forced to feel embarrassed to hear those ugly....letter words.

In fact where our road ends and our compound starts is the free toilet for the pets of the whole colony. Every colony has lumps of dog poop in various hues in front of any corner house. A pet dog maybe the owner's pet or pride, not ours. We don't envy them either.

Coming to the youngsters conducting opinion polls, our colony was an ideal place to conduct such polls. It has lots of strongly opinionated elderly men and women with plenty of spare time. They are extremely enthusiastic about arguments and debates. Someone or the other keeps taking leisurely walks or watering the plants. They might be plucking mangoes or coconuts. It seems to be a woman's prerogative to pluck flowers from their garden or others' gardens. These people would happily take part in the poll. I would have given the young pollster a glass of water or even tea if he gave me a chance to voice my opinion on any topic of public interest to be published in a popular national magazine. My opinion would have been useful to society.

I do imagine so many reasons for the man not coming up to our gate. In the plot next to ours there was a house under construction (it looked like one of his 5 year plans) with mounds of sand, piles of bricks, gravel, scores of rolling wooden poles, and deadly looking iron rods heaped outside 'our' gate. The hurdle they pose could put off any human being. The milkman, the newspaper boy, the Amazon delivery boy and the postman had to deliver and so they came. But an outsider had no such compulsions.

I asked my friend who lived right at the entrance of the colony in house number 1 (ours was 200) whether she had taken part in any such survey. She shook her head rather sadly and said that her own family did not bother about her opinion on anything, why would anyone else ask?

Then I wondered who the people were, who gave their opinion, a 'yes' to be counted in the blue segment, or a 'no' for the red segment, besides 'no comments' and 'can't say' for segments in yellow color.

I could imagine how frustrated a young man must be to carry a heavy file in a shoulder bag asking the same questions again and again. I was sure he would be mostly dismissed with some non-committal answers. Many would say, 'I do not know,' and some people would be rudely asking him to get out.

My elder sister lived in a posh residential colony in the centre of the city. She was an opinionated and experienced person living in a VIP neighbourhood. She has been waiting longer than me to give her precious opinion. But, none ever asked her.

I thought the residents in such upscale areas were perhaps indifferent to such interviews. They would be perpetually on their phones or busy with their various appointments and won't find time for such trivialities. For opinion polls perhaps such surveyors go to the nerve centres of the city like shopping malls, crowded apartment complexes, and to the tech-parks, or nearby parking lots or restaurants.

I called my friend living in one such congested area and she said nobody ever approached her with a questionnaire. She in turn asked her daughter, a working woman whether anyone asked her opinion about working mothers managing the home. Her daughter got very annoyed as she was in a board (boring) meeting and sent her back a rude row of emoji's.

I came to the conclusion that a team of youngsters who get a project to conduct a survey at the last minute, rush to restaurants or wait outside a mall to ask a few youth and a few middle aged people coming out from the theatres or interview a group of frustrated youth searching for jobs. They might not have taken the questions seriously and would give some answers in a light-hearted way, laughing and enjoying the fun. How do we know they had time to analyse the questions and various possible answers!

Of course it all depends on the topic being discussed. We do come across opinion polls conducted on marriages, whether love marriage or arranged marriage works out better. The survey may end up with altogether different answers as there are many options these days. Divorce, living together, remaining single and adopting children, marrying partners of the same sex, so who worries about getting married at all.

It brings us back to the basic question whether opinion polls are found to be essential, whether any serious meaningful research is carried on later or it is just a pastime, a 'casual time pass' as they call it. Maybe it is a feature to fill a few pages in the magazine hurriedly added and they did not have anything better or sensational. It is possible it is nobody's opinion in particular but just a figment of imagination. Ultimately whose opinion is it anyway on anything that we can say is absolutely right?

I'll never know, no one asked me for my opinion.

22

Our New Home - 'House Full' at Last

For us personally a wonder of wonders happened in the late 90's. Incredible as it may seem, we did start the construction of our house on a plot in a cul-de-sac in the same colony in which we bought a plot almost 20 years earlier. We got a smaller plot, drawn by lots again Hmmm.....only a smaller plot seemed to be in our lot.

Many changes had to be made from the original blueprint. Exit and entry could be only through one gate, as the width of the plot was less. There was a storm drain belonging to the corporation which took away a huge chunk from the width of the plot at the end of our road about which we could do nothing. And so the long veranda too was cut short to half its original length and width. The marble flooring became mosaic as not only the costs became high but also our friends advised that marble came with its own list of troubles. It was too slippery and fragile. Leave alone the floor cracking and breaking, we were likely to fall and crack or break our bones. After all, I cannot crawl across the floor like a snake because we have spent too much money on the flooring. Turmeric stains or coffee stains were not easy to get rid off. We cannot cook without turmeric and cannot live without coffee and that too degree coffee from our filter early in the morning. What about tea or pomegranate? That's it., our marble flooring changed to mosaic.

The whole facade had to change as the French window came with its own set of problems. We realised it would only create more work for us seniors. The room may be airy, but along with the air a hoard of mosquitoes would enter from the mango grove and a stagnant Adyar river close by. Letting in too much sunlight in the tropical heat of Madras was perhaps not a great idea. To top it all, who can remove, wash and change 8 panels of 8' long curtains at the age of 70 or 75? The dream home might become a nightmare to maintain. We were 20 years older when we actually constructed the house than what we were when we bought the plot and made the house plan.

Anyway we were thrilled when we walked into the new house in the wee hours of an auspicious day.

The 'grihapravesam', started with the ritual of a cow entering first with a calf in tow. The poor cow was so scared and perhaps could not tread on the polished mosaic and in sheer fear she peed and pooped. The calf followed s...t. "It's okay. It is a good omen," said my quick-witted aunt. Everyone laughed. A funny remark helps to lighten any situation. The guests stopped in their tracks scared of stepping and slipping, as that may not be a good omen.

Hey, come to think of it, I feel, a house is just like the human body. The nervous system being the main switch board with all those thick cables bound at the top like the spinal cord at the neck, then spreading out holding 1, 2, 3, phases, switches, fuses and thinner wires. Compare it to the spinal cord and rib cage. The jet pumps bore well pumps, sump, overhead tank and pipes carrying the water through the length and breadth of the house to the bathrooms and wash basins, sinks etc. form the vascular system. The main pump is the heart, if it stops the whole water supply stops and life comes to a standstill. The sewerage and drainage system is like the gastrointestinal tract and the kidneys which flush out the waste from the human body. The fans and air conditioners are the respiratory system. The walls form the main skeleton. Cracks and seepages are like fractures. Seepages are almost like congenital defects. The doors and windows are the several orifices in our body, which demand timely closing and opening. I feel that the ears and nostrils remaining open forever are like the ventilators in a house.

Soon we settled down happily as we could make new friends in the colony and met our old friends too. Our huge circle of relatives kept us busy because we had to keep attending functions. We started celebrating festivals together with our siblings. We could visit my sisters-in-law, old uncles and aunts and spend lots of time with them. When we lost them subsequently one by one, we considered it a boon for us to have spent time with them when they were hale and hearty. We did not mind the heat and sweat of Madras except when we had day-long power cuts by the TNEB for the sake of maintenance. Did it indicate poor maintenance? What were they maintaining? Were they maintaining the power cuts?

My dream was to have a garden. After planting at least 25 seeds of a tasty mango called 'imam pasand', we saw two saplings grow up nicely into huge healthy trees to give us eventually 100s of fruits within the next 5 to 6 years. They turned out to be everyone's 'pasand'. Out of the 5 coconut saplings we planted, 3 were pulled out by 2 buffalos 1 afternoon. We were literally caught napping. One sapling was attacked by a dangerous bug. The last one survived to wake up after 12 years to yield coconuts. Too late. More coconuts were there when we were not living there anymore. We got sapotas, guavas, papayas and gooseberries besides flowers of sorts. But........we were just two of us living in the house and enjoying the fruits of our labour, not just the fruits but even the spacious dream house itself.

Our sons could not bring their children when they were new-born or even as infants, since travelling before the completion of immunisation shots were considered risky. Imagine 4 grandkids born one after the other in a span of ten years to two different couples. Could they ever plan a trip together? Then at last the suitable time came when they decided to make their visit to stay with us as a complete family and show grandpa's home and their country of origin to their kids.

The whole family getting together was such a rare occurrence that we both were very excited. We bought a new microwave oven, a toaster oven, a water purifier, a new car even and an a/c unit. We were so happy that we went crazy, I think. The house we built for such an occasion was full at last. They all arrived one by one. The grandchildren kept going up and down. They loved the swing. They enjoyed the spicy ribbon 'pakodas', 'murukkus', banana chips, 'bajjis', biscuits, cheese cubes and masala peanuts. The house reverberated with music, laughter and fun. One loved to watch 'Harry Potter' while another wanted to watch 'Star Wars'. The grandson liked only 'planet earth' and other Attenborough movies and yet another liked 'Sherlock Holmes'. The fathers moved with cameras clicking each precious moment. The board games and playing cards were pulled out. Shouts of 'cheating', 'Uno', 'I won, I won,' 'and you are the donkey' could be heard. We simply relished every moment.

Spicy Sambar, rasam and chutneys were okay, but I felt the kids missed Panera sandwiches, pizzas, quesadillas, nachos, tacos, tortillas and pastas a lot. One day after a spell of shopping in a mall we came back with pizzas. But a little girl found a tiny dead cockroach stuck to the lid of one pizza box. It created quite a stir around the dining table. The one who spotted it said she felt sick and ran to the bathroom. She swore she had eaten one. Another saw the olive on the pizza itself and said it was a huge cockroach and she backed out from the table. Another felt her throat felt scratchy. She declared she preferred 'dosas'. Paper-thin crisp dosas, I found no child could resist. Ultimately pizza lost, dosas won.

There was a sudden shower one afternoon. By the evening mosquitoes came in droves as the storm drain outside was blocked. Each one wanted to experiment with the mosquito bats to hunt and kill them. They had a field day hitting mosquitoes with the bat. In fact they enjoyed it most, a game they could only enjoy here in India.

As usual when it rained the power went off. But before the kids could start sweating or being attacked by mosquitoes we had the inverter kicking into action. Of course we could not have the A/C on but at least fans could be switched on. Even that was an experience which they seemed to enjoy immensely.

India is beautiful. Dresses are wonderful. Marina beach was so good. Food is exotic. Jewellery is simply grand. People are so friendly. They loved all these but the trash and potholes on the roads were a bit too much.

They had the taste of India. They loved it, no doubt.

23

Cards You Cannot Discard

The cards that we have to obtain and preserve in our country seem to be increasing year after year. I am referring to the number of utility cards, which are reaching the number 52 (of a pack of cards) slowly and steadily. Husband and wife seem to be the couple of jokers holding the pack. But mind you, we cannot shuffle this pack and play around with them as we wish.

Men and women serving the armed forces get their special identity cards with unique service numbers which each one of the personnel has to carry on his/her person from the day he/she joins the defence service. It becomes a part and parcel of the uniform. The whole family knows the number by heart and are aware of its significance. Come to think of it, the service personnel have to play a lot of 'number games' with their payslips, ration cards, confidential reports, vehicle requirements, etc., which go by numbers only.

After retirement also, the officers carry their ID cards when they go out. I think they get used to carrying this card in their pockets or wallets. It helps them a lot in emergency situations too. Let me explain one such situation. There was a bandh and a huge protest march going on when we were on our way from 'Gangtok' to 'Siliguri' by bus. We had to take our train back to Madras at

Siliguri Station. There were quite a few passengers perhaps in a similar situation to catch a train at Siliguri station. But as luck would have it the bus we were in was very close to an army setup and the driver stopped. My husband, who is a retired senior officer of IAF, could talk to some officer in charge at that army camp about the crisis we were in. The major quickly got a three tonner truck ready and the whole lot of passengers of the bus got in as well and we could take the train to Madras that evening.

Sorry for digressing. But this shows how important an ID card is.

The retired personnel have to make an ECHS (Ex-servicemen's Health Service) card which is absolutely essential for getting treatment in a military hospital or even in any civil hospital they are referred to. It needs to be updated as and when we are asked to do so. As a spouse I need an ECHS card too.

My husband has of course an Air Force Association life membership card. I had to get a membership card of the Air Force Wives Welfare Association, which became mandatory as it would simplify complicated issues if they arise in later life. I have kept it hopefully safe 'somewhere'.

Service personnel require smart cards for canteen facilities. I started wondering whether the card was not that 'smart' after all, as I see my husband renewing it periodically. He says as the rules keep changing, the card has to be updated. As a better half I am there in the photo too as otherwise I cannot use it and I am not even half as smart as him. When it comes to renewing anything I am worse off as the 'worse half', not the so called 'better half'.

The time came I had to get a passport in my name to identify me as an individual. I was happy that at last I had an independent document which would prove I am 'ME'.

I am sorry I forgot the most important card in any citizen's life, which is the Pan Card. Needless to say my husband had a PAN Card for decades. I was a 100% homemaker working without pay, promotions, perks, paid leave etc. Except for a frying pan and a 'dosa' pan I did not have to worry about any other 'PAN', but even I had to make a PAN Card.

Then the government announced an 'Aadhar' card for each citizen of this country. The card is called 'UIDAI', 'Unique Identification Authority of India' card. It is said it would make life easy for us in India (?). For the first time I will be unique numerically too with a 12 digit number. I thought only prisoners while in prison had a unique 'qaidi' number like 420, 720 or whatever.

I did not realise then that it was a huge task to make one and get it linked to every other card or gadget of mine including my cell phone, sewing machine, microwave oven or gas consumer card, but it seems I need to do a lot of linking. I am not surprised though, as I am an Indian and 'Proper connections' do matter here.

This UIDAI card includes my biometric and demographic data. As usual there were and are controversies and opinions galore on the use, abuse, overuse, misuse but ultimately they were of no use. Almost all of them have got their Aadhar card done.

Coming back to my card collection, every card works in one particular area.

There are cards for getting dairy milk packets delivered at the doorstep in the morning. Gas connection comes with a domestic supply card with a number. To book for a refill the consumer should know his/her number by heart, otherwise we cannot book. The latest rule is that the consumer has to go online to book for a refill. The very word 'Online' puts me off completely.

Power supply has a card of course whether it is BESCOM or TNEB (any other electricity board), the meter reading card has to be checked and paid every month, and otherwise the power supply will be terminated.

Making a Civil ration card is mandatory in most of the states. If we shift from one state to another we need a new card all over again. Filling in applications and running around follows. There are gifts galore like fans, grinders, bicycles given free if the elections are around the corner for those who get free rations too. The person who holds the card should be BPL (below poverty line) to obtain these freebies.

A ration card was only accepted as a legal proof of identity earlier. Once, a TTE in a running train asked us to show it as an additional proof of our seniority in age as we had availed 'senior citizen' concession. I was not angry; instead I was happy he took me to be below 60 years in age. I must have looked so young!!!!

Coming to the Driver's license, the laminated license now looks like a card only. I must narrate my experience as to why I gave up my licence long ago when a lamppost suddenly appeared from nowhere in front of my car and to avoid a collision I had to swerve to the right where a huge puddle of water, a small lake, maybe, appeared all of a sudden but thankfully the lamppost moved to its right now and stopped the car with a bang. Oh, no, I was zigzagging. You can imagine if an immobile object like a solid lamp post and a half-dry lake troubled me so much, how I would have managed the moving vehicles and pedestrians on our choc-a-bloc roads. Actually my dreams of driving a car ended with a bang, not with a whimper.

That reminds me my husband has an Automobile Association of India membership card too. In day to day life besides all these we require an ATM card, call it PayTM, Googlepay card or whatever.

Credit cards are great. By all means, 'buy now, pay later,' is tempting but we decided not to fall into the debt trap. But debit cards and credit cards do somehow get into wallets these days for paying online. Thank goodness in our country we can still use hard currency notes, provided all of a sudden, by an overnight announcement they don't go out of circulation due to demonetisation.

That reminds me of elections and politicians. It was the first general election in India after my husband's retirement. While he was in service we only received postal ballots generally after the results of general elections were out.

Post retirement we were thrilled we could exercise our franchise at last as responsible citizens. We applied to get into the voters list and after several rounds of photo and interview sessions, we came out with our 'voter ID cards'. I was standing in a long queue with my head held high outside the polling booth with a voter ID card but the man in charge refused to let me in because he did not find my name in his list. We insisted on going through the list again and there it was my name, on a different page and column. I won my case. Many were turned back rudely. Now I keep the voter cards under lock and key.

Nowadays we keep a stock of passport size and a dozen stamp size ones just in case......someone asks to produce a document. The passport size photographs are bad enough as one has to look serious and glum. But nothing can beat the ghastly black biometric photo taken for 'Aadhaar'. It looked more ghostly and ghastly than an old negative.

My great grandfather left behind just one photograph of him for posterity as he was scared of getting his lifespan reduced by being photographed. But here I am leaving a picture of my brain, spine, my entire skeleton (I am referring to X-rays, scans, MRI's) and even of my iris. The image of the iris is scary as I look like a cat. My grandchildren might think they had feline ancestry. We leave our photos behind in all public places, passport offices, banks, hospitals, CCTV cameras, besides social media, and everywhere else, except (hopefully) not in police stations.

I used to think I had no identity of my own except as 'Mrs. Rama' or 'Chhotu ki ma' in Air Force quarters, but now I have a pack of cards to prove that I am no nonentity but a woman with a million identities.

24

The Most Populous Democracy

On 11th May 2000 CE India's population officially reached the milestone of one billion. The billionth baby chosen by the authorities was a healthy baby girl born early in the morning in a hospital in New Delhi. More babies arrived just before her or around the same time along with her or a minute after her elsewhere. Remember there were babies born at the rate of 30 per minute. But she was lucky to be chosen as the 'one billionth person' who made the historic moment. This is what the newspaper I was browsing through in the dentist's waiting room reported then. I just happen to remember this.

I reflected on this when there was the news in the papers recently about our country becoming the number 1 nation population-wise overtaking China. From 340 million at the time of independence in 1947 zooming to a billion in the year 2000 seemed quite an achievement indeed. An addition of 66 millions in 53 years seemed unbelievable. "We two, ours two" the family planning slogan was introduced in 1952 and it did not seem to have had much effect after all. Perhaps there were a lot of 'accidental babies 'born.

Now by the year 2023 CE, we have added 40 million more to the 1 billion and we have already become the number one nation 'population wise'. The good news is that India has 65% of its population below 35 years of age. The average age is said to be 29 while in other countries it is much higher. That means we are a young nation 'average age wise'. And as a democratic republic free from colonial rulers our nation is just 75 years old. For a nation 75 is young but for us humans it is considered almost the fag end with one foot down in the grave. Let us not forget that as a civilization, we are one of the most ancient and the only one carrying on civilization and culture in all its glory, while the other ancient ones are just not there anymore. We should be proud as India is the most populous 'democratic republic' in the world. Wow, 'democratic republic 'is the term we have to be happy and proud about.

No wonder, you see people, people everywhere and unfortunately not water, water everywhere, except during the monsoon when we see our flooded roads running like rivers.

I go down memory lane. I grew up in Madras of the good old days in the late 40s when the Marina Beach was the second longest natural beach in the world. It looked so serene and calm that one could hear only the non-stop roar of the waves rising and lashing against the shoreline. There was an endless expanse of clean golden sands for miles together. Now the beach and the road running along the coast in Chennai are so overcrowded with hundreds of people shopping. There are shops running from the main road to the shoreline that the sands are not visible even. Hundreds of cars are parked all over the place. The old charm is not there. The boundless spread of the cobalt blue waters met the clear blue sky at the horizon and the foamy waves splashed against the swathes of golden sands in the front. But somehow the sea and sandy stretches seem to have lost their limitless space. They look so congested with memorials, swimming pools, shops and what not. The vastness is lost. There is the din, hustle and bustle of people thronging to the beaches for fun, eating and sightseeing. It is sad to see the springy, spongy and smooth sands trashed beyond belief.

Even in the 50's there was hardly any vehicular traffic on the beach road except a few city buses, cars and cabs going to the high court, Mount Road, central Station or the Madras harbour. But now the volume of traffic is so heavy that even the sea breeze instead of ozone might carry Co2.

The age old 'Santhome' Church right on the seashore along with scores of ancient temples in Mylapore, Triplicane, Tiruvanmiyur, George Town and the popular mosque in Triplicane, might have always had devotees visiting them but now devotees have to stand in mile long queues pushing each other because everyone seems to be in a hurry.

Take the cinema theatre. Back in our youth a small building consisting of two floors stood by itself running three shows a day except on Sundays when there would be a morning show. Now a multiplex of a handful of theatres on the topmost floor of the mall running three to four shows, a food court on the same floor, showrooms and outlets of branded products on another level or two and a huge parking lot in the basement, stand as a part of a mega mall attracting thousands of people. It is said that some are actually shopping; a majority are browsing and a few perhaps shoplifting. It seems the crowds indicate a booming economy. The sea of people seemingly pushing around on the pavements on the roads might look chaotic but they are all moving towards their destination.

Boom time or recession we have millions out there buying things in the vegetable and fruit markets and grocery shops every minute round the clock 24 x 365. The 30 babies born every minute in the country naturally have to share the same land, air, water, sky, sun and moon. So the sellers are selling and the buyers buy as they need the things to survive.

We have millions of men and women striking deals to buy vehicles of sorts every minute in some city, town or village. They will have to share the same potholed roads which are already choc-a block with traffic. I wish someone seriously makes flying cars like the ones we see in cartoons.

There is maximum demand for affordable 2 BHK flats mostly in the outskirts of the cities. They are the middle class who have to live and make their living. So the good news is we have citizens who have the money to buy houses.

At the other end of the spectrum we see the very rich and famous, a minuscule percentage of our huge population. They are forever buying the latest automobiles, private planes, yachts, antiques, designer garments, Royal beds, golden faucets and other bathroom fixtures, diamond studded jewellery made of platinum. We are indeed fortunate to have such billionaires living among us otherwise; our BMW's, MERCs, Lamborghinis, Toyotas and Rolls Royce's will remain parked in the showrooms. They make our country rich provided they stay here and pay their taxes.

The upwardly mobile keep updating their mobile phones too from basic to feature phones to smartphones and onto the latest iPhones. No wonder every other shop in any shopping centre is selling cell phones. Do we see anyone walking on the road without a mobile phone?

Leave alone the crowded metropolises, the hill stations which were cool and airy are so congested now as they have to accommodate more tourists and more residents. The domestic travelling schedules are heavy now as the middle class travel a lot. Good business is good for the country but the hill stations have built houses and hotels down the slopes. When 'Kedarnath' was hit by the cloudburst, such dwellings crumbled and slid down killing the trapped tourists and residents. In major cities the heritage structures which stood in the midst of spacious gardens have disappeared or they are buried deep in the midst of flyovers, metro-rail tracks, office complexes, and malls. They have to be spotted with great difficulty. Naturally they are obvious signs of progress.

The country has only this much land and so it can develop only as much as it can support. Perhaps we should have planned for more smart cities earlier. These satellite townships with all amenities would have been so good to the overall development of the country too.

But let us look at the plus points of overpopulation. Whatever anyone may say, India is a very rich country with a huge repository of gold. Even the not-so rich people give their daughters gold jewels at the time of their marriage. Tons of gold is being bought for millions of girls born and getting married somewhere or the other in the country every day. Wow. That is a hell of a lot of gold!

We have a youthful population to join our armed forces, security and police forces. We have highly qualified engineers to manage our Railways. We have millions to serve as engineers in the armed forces, engineers to run our factories, industries and other manufacturing units. We have doctors and nurses to run our hospitals; we have professors and teachers to teach in our educational institutions. Foremost we have farmers to cultivate our food grains and other crops. If Indians work hard and put in their best efforts, the slogan, making for India and for the world will not be an impossible task. We can do it.

Anyone who excels in sports can win medals of gold, silver or bronze now. Our sportsmen and women have achieved great success in international sporting events whether it is an individual game or a team game. Men and women have performed so well in boxing, wrestling, weight lifting, shooting, javelin throw, badminton and tennis etc. and won acclaim and honours in recent years. Women have done so well in the world of women's cricket. Our huge population still has many more untapped talents!!!

Oscar's seemed to be out of reach but this year even at Oscar's a documentary film produced in India won the award. This year for the first time the soundtrack from a Telugu cinema RRR won an award for the most original song. Actually we could get many more awards as the number of movies made in India run into thousands and the number of songs runs into millions.

We still have people to partake in political rallies and join protest marches on city roads. Hundreds of volunteers rush to any natural disaster sites and render their service during rescue operations while still there are those who can remain passive onlookers. There are those rowdy elements who steal from the injured or dead too.

The din and noise all around makes us happy and cheerful. Void is like absolute emptiness in life. Of what use is a stadium without spectators, a theatre without an audience, or a train without passengers, or roads without pedestrians? That would be like ghost towns we see of war - torn cities on the small or big screen.

People indicate life. Millions of youth are a real boon and blessing to us. Let's get together and work together to make our country great and the real number one in the world!

People throng to the temple festivals and to the beach and to the shops by cars and autos. And so we have people, people everywhere

Temple Chariot Festival.

Shopping on the Beach!

Traffic who will take the car out first?

25

The Monsoon Mayhem

When we were small I remember after a heavy rain we used to make paper boats and leave them in the stream of shallow water running on both sides of the road. There were no actual storm drains but water never stagnated that much. Was the laying of the roads good or the sloping was perfect? Maybe the volume of plastic trash, thermocol, bubble wraps huge cartons and debris of sorts were absent and so the water flowed freely without any hurdle.

Monsoon in India is said to be very unique. It is an enormous movement of water and energy travelling through many oceans in the direction of the wind. When a depression forms in the bay, the black clouds condense. Thunder and lightning announce the approaching downpour and it pours and pours. In the month of June, in fact on the 1st of June, as it mostly happens, the southwest monsoon hits Kerala and the much awaited rains in our subcontinent start, after months of heat and dust. The trees happily wash off the whole lot of dust from their branches. The wet green leaves glisten beautifully when the sun comes out after the rains. The dried up lakes and rivers get their fill up to the gills ready to overflow any minute. Should I add, provided they have not been plotted and allotted to builders during the dry months.

When the monsoon starts in our country, the mood of people is upbeat as it comes after a long spell of tropical heat with the mercury touching even 50 degree C. The joy turns to panic and anxiety when they step out on the roads on day 2 or 3 after a non-stop downpour. That is when they come to wade through in the waist deep and chest deep water.

"It has never rained like this in the past 100 years," the reports would declare. It annoys the public more than any other statement. But they don't even say, hey, even last year you made the same remark. Perhaps the reporters are only worried about that day's crimes and other cases. Immediate rescue operations are carried out by the local able-bodied youth to evacuate the older marooned people in the neighbourhood moving them to a higher level, I mean physically to a shelter at a higher or drier level. Then after a day or more the authorities enter into full-fledged operations to arrange for a vacant school building or some such place for the stranded people and provide them food. Of course we have to agree that disaster management is a gargantuan task as the rescuing team has to cross the same river on the roads.

After the downpour stops when life seems to wade or sail back to normalcy slowly, with the victimised people picking up whatever they could retrieve from the slush, the blame game starts and goes on and on.

The citizens proclaim loudly "storm drains were not cleared for ages". Too late, he should have cried from his rooftop earlier.

"You people dump the whole lot of packing material of your fridge or washing machine including the cartons, bubble wrap and thermocol in the storm drain. Ask your neighbours what they did last week", the local counsellor would shout at the top of his voice.

"Do you see the ramps on the main road covering the storm drains," his fury was more than the fury of the rains.

True, people don't bother to leave the storm drains accessible for removing debris even.

"Lakes and ponds were used up to build our houses and I bought my flat, now it is under water and I am on the road," one woman would cry complaining to the TV crew. It seems when she bought the plot she did not know it was a lake originally which was temporarily filled with rubble sand or whatever and sold. The crowd around her would give her all the vocal support. They are all from the same submerged apartment complex.

This question remains unanswered.

Another point put up by the citizens. "Garbage was not collected and of course, "the roads had not been repaired for ages". "Even manholes were open in several places, which caused accidents", they yell in their regional language to the TV crew interviewing them. The same complaints in every town and city all over the country.

Ultimately the rains die down on their own when the clouds move to wreak havoc elsewhere. Though it is unbelievable, within weeks people forget and move on with their lives. They have to, life's like that.

We only come to know about the horrendous havoc hit the people from the visuals on TV. The journalist in charge of flood scenes from that area is interviewing them, busily asking the same questions again and again. Only the answers come in a different language depending on which part of the country is hit. The Minister's argument is "Even Houston looked the same when the hurricane hit. When hurricane Irma hit Florida, it was a complete disaster with the power failure lasting for several days," the men in power remark.

True, the visuals are similar except the houses and the people looked very different. But I wonder whether a category 6 hurricane and expected monsoon rains belong to the same category?

People can escape the severe heat, the severe chill, by staying indoors. But is it humanly possible to stop the gushing flood waters from rushing in with a shovel or a bucket? Can they ever save their things which just float out in front of their eyes?

Scientists and researchers say the citizens of the world are responsible for climate change. We had a green planet to start with but we chopped the trees, we burnt the fossil wood, we buried the lakes with high rise structures, we drained the oil from the depths of the earth to run our vehicles 24 x 7, we filled the atmosphere with CO2. To top it all we filled the earth with non-degradable trash. The protective gases like ozone and oxygen are depleting. We have warmed up our own Mother Earth. Our children will face the dire consequences. How sad it is! Can we still prevent any such eventuality and the 'monsoon mayhem'?

Yes, it is very much a 'Mission possible'.

26

The Deluge

The year 2015 was coming to an end. Weathermen on TV channels came out with daily bulletins about the torrential rains in certain areas along the east coast and the formation of further depressions in the bay moving towards the southern part of the peninsula etc. In short the northeast monsoon was extremely active bringing copious rains in the southern states of Tamilnadu, Andhra Pradesh, and Karnataka. We usually listen to the weather forecast especially during the northeast monsoon as it hits our daily lives directly and more severely because we were living close to the Adyar river. In the month of October itself there were heavy rains all over Tamil Nadu especially in the city of Chennai and surrounding areas.

A couple of years after we moved to Chennai, around 2004 the rains were quite heavy and we had a sample of the Adyar River overflowing onto the streets. Our neighbour said that the trouble was the river was unable to drain the surplus water fast enough into the sea when they released more water from the huge reservoir at 'Chembarambakkam'. He said that it was reported that the riverbed had not been desilted and cleaned for ages and hence the water could not flow down into the sea. It resulted in a backlash.

Once again in the year 2010, the surplus water released from the reservoir at Chembarambakkam flooded our roads to chest-deep level. But the next day it all cleared. We were slightly upset but very soon we forgot the incident. After that it was all fine. We moved on and somehow we thought that was not going to happen ever again.

Yet another monsoon arrived bringing heavy downpour every now and then. It was the year 2015. On 15th and 16th of Nov that year, we had my niece and her husband staying with us. Fortunately our guests could take the flight to reach Bengaluru on 16th evening in time to catch the flight the next morning to go back home to the USA. Had it been the next day they could not have left our house in Chennai!

Next day, the 17th November 2015, there was a non-stop rain. There was waist-deep water stagnating around the house and we could see many cobras swimming gracefully in their glistening golden coats in the storm drains by the side of our house.

But the stagnant water cleared up the next day after more than 36 hours. But perhaps the monsoon was not exactly over as the sky remained overcast quite often. A series of depressions started forming in the bay and it rained on and off the next few days. Yet another seemingly non-stop downpour had started on the 30th evening with terrible thunder and lightning and continued through the night. We spent a sleepless night.

Did the IMD know it was going to be a very heavy rainfall the next day, which was the 1st Dec 2015? Had NASA warned our Met dept. of a non-stop downpour of more than 100cms on that single day? Oh, God. We were told all this after the deluge was over.

The sluice gates of the Chembarambakkam reservoir were not opened to make room for the incoming rainwater. Perhaps they were saving water for the following summer as they would be blamed if a scarcity of water arose. The Adyar river was flowing at the normal level the preceding week or so. This report about the water level in the river was given by our domestic help (not by met. department). She lived bang on the bank of Adyar. The optimists that we were we thought the authorities might have done some clearing up at the estuary where Adyar river meets the sea..

Day 1

It was the 1st of Dec. Early in the morning it was pouring as though the sky was torn and someone poured bucketful's of water through the tear. In addition to the torrential rains, during the course of the day two other reservoirs around the city were opened as they were all filled up to the gills. This we heard on TV around 11am. After that our power supply went off many times. There was no warning and no announcement given to the public to be watchful about more water getting released. We heard a couple of hours later from my sister-in-law living elsewhere in the city, where it was raining but the roads were not so badly flooded. She said that she heard a report that a river unknown to us till then, called 'Kosasthalai' brought in more water from outside the city. To top it she said that some water might be released from Chembarambakkam reservoir but the weather bulletin did not specify how many cusecs of water would be released.

The noise of the rain which came in sheets was unbearable.

There was no power supply and hence no television for us. There was no way of getting the latest report on anything happening on the waterfront. The landlines for telephones were not working. We started feeling cut off from the outside world. We did not have any neighbours close to us. One who was there was not to be seen at all, from the previous day itself. There was no way of getting any updates whatsoever, unless the police went around on the streets making announcements on loudspeakers. But there was no sign of any such announcement. The noise was terrible and scary. We had never seen rain like that. Why did they not tell us whether they were opening the sluice gates also?

It was around 6pm. We thought we would have an early dinner but the lumps in our throats did not allow the food to go down the gullet. We washed our hands and put the cooked food in the fridge. We even had fruits and plenty of eats etc. on the dinner table. But we did not feel like eating anything at all. We looked around us in the living room. We had sent our only help 'the maid' home as she had to take care of her house and children. There were so many things that we had to save from the water if it entered our premises. The only way to save them would be to carry them upstairs to the first floor. But who can carry heavy things and climb the steps too? My husband picked up some hard cash, his wallet, watch and a few more things. We were dazed, our hands and legs felt limp. We seemed so weak, drained of all energy.

We lived on the ground floor with all our worldly possessions like most people do, especially the seniors. On the first floor was my husband's study with a desktop computer and its accessories like a printer, scanner, speakers, and camera. Etc. Our lifeline, an almirah with very important documents, was there too. The other bedroom had guest beds and a steel almirah with bed linen. Thankfully, a huge collection of our books was in an almirah upstairs in the landing space. Then there was an open terrace. We could not fill the overhead tank with clean water after the morning of 30 th Nov. There was an overhead tank on the terrace on the second floor. Since the sump and the open well would surely be mixed with the filthiest water from all around the city we did not want to pump any water even when the power was there the previous evening.

There were so many collections of ours as we were nearing 50 years of our married life. These things were all around us like precious family photographs in frames, CDs, video cassettes of 60th and 80th birthday celebrations of parents, weddings of our sons, and audio cassettes of all types of music from classical to 'Indie pop'. I picked some from the wooden cupboard there and placed them on a curio shelf at a height of 7 feet. I thought that should be a safe height to escape inundation. The DVD player, the New Sony TV, 'Tanjore' paintings, oil paintings, batiks, wall hangings (all handmade), curios, Air Force mementos, keepsake souvenirs collected from memorable visits were on display all around. My eyes went around the room. I could go on and on about gadgets like our fridge, brand new microwave oven, an 'oven toaster grill', washing machine, grinder, mixie, a water purifier RO type, No, we cannot save a thing. It was too late. We had none to help us. The minute the rain became heavier and since my sister-in-law told us they might open the reservoir we had sent our only help away. It was over. I could cry aloud and nobody can hear. No one can come for help.

I went up to run to the open terrace to show myself to the helicopter flying overhead. But no, I could see people in the copter but in all probability they did not see me.

We packed whatever jewels were at home and hard cash that we could manage to carry up in a purse earlier. Thank God for it. Fortunately we could take 4 or 5 bottles of water, a packet of biscuits and a small bunch of bananas, which was going to sustain us for the next 48 hours. Now that was that. We can do nothing more. We were frozen. We could only carry ourselves up holding our Pooja 'mandap', a few idols, oil lamps, and framed pictures of gods from our Pooja room. Now we can only pray to God to save us from the ugly dirty water flooding our house. My legs felt limp like a ragdoll and my husband had to do most of the climbing.

Thank god I did a few things before the water seeped in. I managed to put the entire ready to eat snacks on the top most shelves in the kitchen cupboard. I felt thrilled with every little thoughtful (?) move I made in semi-darkness. I did put a couple of cameras, watches and some silverware inside the locker of the steel almirah. "The locker closes 'air tight'; water cannot seep in, is it not?" I asked my husband. He just nodded his head. I don't think he could hear my choked voice even. We left a suitcase full of silk saris above the almirah say more than 7 feet high or so. These we could not carry up. We told each other "That much water will never come inside". How could we be so sure and why were we so sure?

I came down the steps for the eighth time that evening. I looked sadly at the fat tomes on my table. I saw the dictionaries, Thesaurus, and a lot of other voluminous books there. A laptop with a network of entangled wires could not be separated in darkness. I did not realise that I was seeing all these for the last time. Two precious manuals containing the names of all awardees of various medals of Indian Air Force of the past seven to eight decades up to 2014 CE were there. My husband's name with all the details of his meritorious service for winning the'Vishisht Seva Medal' in the year 1987 was in the manual. The medal itself was in the almirah. The parchment with the citation signed by the President of India and a precious photograph were hanging on the wall. It was all heavy. We did not know that it would go under water within the next few hours.

We were shocked when my husband switched on the small torchlight in his hand on the thin sheet of water. Yes, the water was glistening. There we were standing on the mid-level landing space of our semi spiral staircase helplessly watching the water creeping in under the front door. It was dark, pitch dark. We had two small flashlights as our sources of light. The possibility of snakes crawling in was there. Within minutes there would be water under the inverter. My husband had to save it from soaking. After all, tomorrow was 'another day' and the inverter might be handy in the absence of a long spell of power failure. We did not have an inkling of what was in store for us! My husband managed to save it.

He got down the stairs to pick up some shirts, trousers next, which were out there hanging in the hangers on the stand. But the minute he put his foot down on the ground he slipped and fell. I cried aloud, "I said, we don't want to save anything, come up please, "I screamed almost. He came up and we both sat on the bed. We were tired, too tired. I stretched my legs. Tears rolled down my cheeks. He said," don't cry now, call my sister and ask her what the news says", But the cell phone was dead. Our last contact with the world outside was gone.

It was around 10pm. The cell phone did not work. The tower must have been submerged. Oh, no!!! We were just sitting on our beds restlessly. Every other minute we went to the top of the staircase to observe the water rising step by step. I could not even cry though I felt like crying aloud. I just could not. My mouth went dry; maybe my eyes went dry too.

Day 2

By the early morning of 2ndDec, the entire ground floor looked like a dirty pond. A gas cylinder was banging against the wall of the staircase. Various things made strange gurgling noises. The 14th step of the staircase was covered by 9am. On 2nd Dec. There was a landing space there. By 3pm. it had covered the 20th step. The rain we saw that day we had never seen in our long lives. Only the last step was left dry. If the level of water rose anymore it would enter our first floor. That would be the end. Water was rippling near the bedroom window upstairs where the a/c unit was kept, ready to flow in any minute. There was water threatening to enter from the front open terrace. It looked like a whirlpool going in circles carrying innumerable things including animals all around. Were they carcasses? We could not make out. We kept running between the front open terrace to the back terrace in sheer desperation. In the hope that a helicopter might spot us.

Around 4 pm on 2nd Dec. Some young boys, actually they were workers who were engaged in constructing a big house behind ours saw us. They were standing near a brick wall in the half built house looking out. That house which was under construction was at a 45 degree angle to ours. They started talking to us. One of them, their leader obviously, offered to take us across a bridge he would construct to the second floor in their building so that we could escape the flood on our first floor if it came that day. He said they heard more water was getting released and coming into the city from the outskirts. Oh God, no, no we cannot take any more of that. The ‘bridge ‘idea was good but was it feasible? We were two septuagenarians and I was an arthritis patient. I could not walk straight on a smooth level road. There was a sea of water all around us.

But they were insistent. On his own that boy started fabricating a bridge with a few 'ballies' and coir ropes, standing in the scaffolding with more than 20 to 25 feet of water gushing all around him. One more boy helped him. That neighbouring plot had been dug for laying a foundation for a huge bungalow and that pit added 10 or more feet of water. He said that it was not safe for us to stay in our house all alone. No boat or help would come as our house was at the end of the colony in a cul-de-sac. He finished making the bridge within 30 minutes. It was unbelievable that we walked over the rickety bridge with his help of course, and reached their quarters on the second floor after 30 minutes. It was dark and depressing. The rain was pouring. We were drenched. I still don't know how we made it. The bridge was on two levels. The poor boy held my arms in a strong grip so that I wouldn't slip and fall. There was one more boy behind him. I had to jump and get on to the second level. After that my arms pained for many days, that much care he took to see that I won't fall. After I reached their house, he came back and brought my husband holding his arms too in a strong grip. The boys took a plastic chair and two bed sheets and pillows.

That night, there we were lying on a wet muddy flooring covered with a wet tarpaulin. We were trying to sleep surrounded by a dozen complete strangers and we were getting drenched in the rain splashing from the wide open gaping window to my left. The thin sheet could not help us much. It was a deluge out there. Needless to add we were literally shivering. It was the month of December, remember, even Chennai gets cold in that month. We were shivering, absolutely shaken by all the unexpected, uncontrollable turns and twists of events taking place. How could we sleep? I was so shocked that even my tears had dried up. Maybe the tear glands were frozen. I had never imagined in my wildest dreams that this state will come to us ever.

Day 3

We were waiting for the daylight to break. There was no bathroom except for some walls. It was terrible really.

On the morning of 3rd Dec. The rain was less intense but the surrounding water level remained the same. Thankfully the level did not rise. Our first floor was safe to go to. We had to go there as the half-built house had no proper flooring, no water connection, no toilets, no doors, no windows, nothing in fact except the plastered walls and the ceiling and the kind-hearted boys. A couple of them took us back again. We gave them money and thanked them profusely. Any amount of money could not have brought anyone to rescue us that day. We ran to the bathroom to wash and brush.

By noon the contractor asked these workers to leave for their homes as no work would be done for the next fortnight at least. They had to pack and leave as they had no job and hence no pay and no food. This was a bad turn for us. We needed their help as we did not know what was in store for us. But they had to go. They gave some hot cooked rice before they left. That plain rice was our lunch that day.

At the end of the third day we realised we were just left with two sets of daily wear for each of us. They were drying inside the room upstairs on a temporary clothesline tied by our maid that morning. The rest of the clothes were ruined in the 'steel almirahs' downstairs getting filled with dirty water from all over the city. By now we were even beyond crying.

To cut the long story short we crossed the same bridge twice more in the next 24 hours with the help of some other workers. That evening of 3rd Dec. after 72 hours of isolation, we got into a boat which could sail in the street behind us for which we had to walk on the shaky bridge again. No boat would dare come to our street which still had the flood waters swirling around in great force. It was getting dark.

When we did leave after almost three days of complete marooned state and near starvation we did not know where to go. The boat left us on the main road. A Good Samaritan helping people to go to the next main road to get some transport took us also in his car. We thanked God when this gentleman too appeared from nowhere and said he lived in Adyar where my sister-in-law law lived. He said there the roads were still motor-able. It was ironical that while the suburb Adyar was okay, the river Adyar had submerged all our houses in our colony. But once again we got one more person sent by God to rescue us at the right time at the right place. The deluge was too much to handle at the age of 70 +.

We were overwhelmed when we saw our sister-in-law open the door for us. When we contacted our children abroad they were so relieved. “Oh, God, at last we hear your voices. You both are safe. We tried desperately to contact you but none knew where you were. We could not find out anything about you and your “well-being”, they said in voices choked with emotion. They had come to know of a tragic incident in our colony from Social Media. A couple got locked in the ground floor of their house and drowned in the flood waters without help as none could even approach their house and open it.

The next day we left Chennai by taxi. It was decided that we would go to Coimbatore to get over the shock. When we came back after a week or so we stayed with our friends in a drier location in the city. But for our niece’s husband’s help we could not have gotten back to Chennai even then. He worked with a team of people to retrieve our precious possessions which could be picked up from the dirty slush inside the house. It took a week for him to just make a way for us to enter and see our house in absolute shambles. Everything was on the floor. Whatever could be saved and cleaned was saved. He supervised the whole operation and sorted out things. But most of the things were lost, broken or untraceable except the stainless steel and brassware etc. They were kitchenware, containers and utensils. Even those I had to get them re-polished as I was not comfortable using them in that state. The clothes inside the almirahs were slushy and stinking and were given away to those who wanted them. I did not see most of them. We did not even know how many precious letters, books, photos, Video cassettes, batiks, Tanjore paintings all made by me and a million other things like air force uniforms, ceremonial ones, peak cap, medals, keepsakes, souvenirs, collections we lost because they were beyond repair.

. Needless to add we spent more money on cleaning, restoring and renewing the house in the next three months. All electrical and electronic gadgets died. Car had to be junked. Home appliances had to be just given away to anyone who wanted them. We continued to live there for nearly a year, but the impact of the flood remained deeply ingrained in my brain. I could never get over the trauma.

Yes, the deluge taught us detachment to material things. In a way it helped us to declutter. But we lost irreplaceable treasures. How in a situation like that help came from absolute strangers who were so kind and compassionate, so eager to help an old couple was amazing. When I was pushed in a corner, I was able to muster up courage to climb, jump, do a pole walk and stay shivering and hungry for 15 hours. We slept surrounded by complete strangers. Yes, we could not get bogged down and sink in the sewage water but had to swim and come out as though nothing ever happened to us.

God Almighty wanted to teach us some lessons on detachment to material things.

Utter chaos after the deluge

The Flimsy' Bridge'

The havoc wreaked by the flood

27

The Wonder Kids of 21st Century

I am unable to cope up with the speed at which our technology advances. This seems more so in the field of computers. I mean even we, seniors handle iPads and cell phones. And every day there is a new term added to this computer jargon. I should at least be able to differentiate between Twitter, Instagram, Telegram, iOS, Android, Chat, Snapchat, and ChatGPT and so on and so forth. The kids of today are so fast and smart at picking up any terminology and working on their electronic devices. Take typing a message on the cell phone for instance. You must have observed how fast today's kids type on the keyboard, even on the tiny keyboard of a smartphone. Their fingertips just glide by, their left thumbs manage most of the typing. When they use both their thumbs they are super-fast. Left or right, I can never type right as my plump thumb goes and sits plum on two or three alphabets straight. Little finger is little better. The index finger is worse. Thanks to arthritis, not one finger is straight; each tip faces a different direction. If I try to press 'O' with my index finger, it touches 'P'. If I try to be fast, my clumsy fingers type 'L's and 'O's in a row. I end up typing 'loo's' and 'pees'. In between the autocorrect will type its own text. If I don't check the message before sending, the words 'autocorrected' can break relationships and friendships.

Let me explain. The other day I started typing a message to my friend. I had typed just two letters 'G' and 'O' to type the name 'Gopi'. The word it completed was Gorilla. Honestly I did not see this before sending it. Her son Gopi got so angry as the text on the tiny screen read as 'How is my 'dear 'Gorilla'. My dear friend, his mother, got so upset that she stopped sending me messages, not even forwards. I had to explain and apologise to her a million times over the phone as she cut me off completely. In fact I told her several times I was not aware of the autocorrected 'gorilla 'in the message. She was my good friend. I felt miserable as I was missing posts with video clippings (both true and fake). What's life without WhatsApp!!! I had to get back into the group chat.

On another occasion, I was going to compliment yet another friend that the orange suit she was wearing in her profile photo was looking nice on her, but the message I sent appeared like this, 'you look nice in the Orangutan suit'. My goodness, it became a huge issue. I am very careful with my posts nowadays.

Let me come back to 'chats' on cell phones again. My granddaughter finishes planning a shopping programme with her friend about which mall they should go to, who will take the car, what they want to buy, at what time they want to leave and where they will meet in the mall, in a minute in 25 to 30 chat messages. She showed it to me because I asked her. I was stunned.

The messages looked indecipherable to me. There were just alphabets, numerals, punctuation marks and emoticons.

"?. I? ICU', 'TQ,' 'LMK', '2F4U', b4, 'B2K', 'BBC'. 'U2', :-)))), WRU :(....OMG. U2... AKA, BTW, CYA." There was not even one complete word, leave alone sentences.

Another granddaughter says emoticons, especially the smileys, convey a range of emotions beautifully. I told her, "These smileys remind me of my dance teacher who taught me Bharatanatyam, a dance form of South India. I was taught to express a range of nine major emotions, with my mouth and eyes. I had to learn how to show happiness, sadness, indifference, surprise, love, hatred, fear, shock and disgust". "Quite a task it was", I told her.

"But see, how effortlessly the smiley does that, it's so easy, grandma," said my nine year old granddaughter. "Emojis can express what words cannot. You can see the feelings visually", she said in an emotional voice and a smiling face imitating a 'smiley'. I loved her excitement and expression.

Yesterday she told me, "Years back (?) my friends and I used to chat using mostly smiley faces and 'emoji's'. Now I don't. Some of my friends connect only on 'Tik-Tok', Snapchat and Instagram with pictures and videos. When they meet they don't 'talk' but they believe in Tik-Tok. They love to check Facebook or Twitter every 10 minutes" she said. The best was when she declared she needed a break from social media. What? Really?

When I read about the latest Melting face, the saluting face, and the dotted line face, I called her. "Yes, I know. I love them," she said in an excited way.

I asked her, "Does that mean you are back to texting?" She just showed thumbs up icon.

I imagined what a chat would look like in the future. Will it be like hieroglyphics or etchings on the wall by 'Neanderthals?' The difference being while birds and animals typed on mobiles and tablets just flash across and can be deleted, Egyptians carved them on stone tablets to remain forever.

On the whole a tiny smartphone is the only tool or device today's kids need for education, information, communication &

entertainment. All the notes that they take are in a chrome book or laptop. I think very soon the notebooks, pencils, pens, erasers, files, staplers and gem clips will disappear.

OMG, the stationary shops might close shop. We seniors still need them all.

Ask them anything except their name, perhaps, the children look at the smartphone. They would go by the rating given by the rotten tomato for the latest Bollywood flick '*Yeh Kutta kis kamineka hain?*' or which pizza outlet gives the authentic (Indian) pizza with 'channa', cheese, olives and desi 'garam' masala for a spicy touch. Google is their guru. Wikipedia is their 'acharya'. YouTube is the tutor in flesh and blood and cursor is the guiding light.

The real teachers in flesh and blood are virtually non-existent!!!

Not only my grandchildren, even my husband is online all the time. He is forever paying bills online. If not that, he is browsing, shopping, banking, linking 'Aadhar' to yet another device, renewing FDs, checking his pension account, updating his passbook, recharging mobiles or filling up forms of sorts for taxes of sorts. When our sons call to speak, they seem to be multitasking too. While talking on the phone, one son is checking his emails, messages, or tracking some important spare parts which he must have ordered for the dishwasher. He simultaneously keeps searching for the best rated dishwasher, which they may have to eventually buy. "Bye, amma, I have to pick up a conference call", our call gets disconnected. Another son says he has taken a short break from a meeting. He has to go and join a zoom meeting. The daughters-in-law are ordering groceries or gifts online, while the granddaughter is coding online. Grandson is busy with his blog or app he is making. Yet another girl is doing a huge project work online researching various websites. One is busy 'spotifying' her favourite songs.

Ugh.... When everyone masters the art of doing everything online in no time, here I am going off the track and derailing every other minute. My husband would choose a new password every day to keep the hackers away. The computer would ask, 'forgot the password, "and once again I repeat. But it says it is the 'wrong password' again. Once more I used the wrong password, it failed and disappeared.... I did not know what to do.

My husband walked in. He asked, "What have you done? You have crashed the computer. I have to reboot all over again. You cannot handle all this. Forget it," he took control of the mouse.

Not just the kids, the whole family are tech-savvy and live in the virtual world. I am left alone to roam around in the real world.

For hours on end they play on the console

28

From Gen A to Z

It is very interesting to read about the nomenclature given to various generations born in America in the past hundred and twenty years. It is said that between Gen 1, called the greatest generation, (born between 1901 to 1924) and Gen Z born after 1996, there are four generations. I was curious to know about the one called the Silent Gen, who is said to be the Gen born between 1925 to 1945. It seems ironic indeed as the generation which experienced the most deadly battles with deafening gunshots, zooming aircrafts bombarding cities, chugging and puffing steam engines carrying loads of screaming victims to the gas chambers, and ultimately the atomic bombs destroying two cities in Japan (boooooom.........followed by deathly silence). They are said to belong to silent Gen! The reason, I came to know later, is said to be that the children born in this era were only seen, not heard. Oh, perhaps in the sense they had no chance to voice their opinions. Once the war was over, the immigrants settling down in the USA became quiet and were determined to work hard for the country's progress and their own livelihood. Hence the term 'silent' is used to denote them. Anyway I remain confused as the dates and definitions keep varying from one source to the other.

They were sure about one generation, which was that of the Baby boomers born between 1946 to 1964. It is said after the war, there was a sudden spurt in the number of babies born. Perhaps there was peace and hope in the very atmosphere that people relaxed and enjoyed. It resulted in the birth of babies. But after the baby boomers, the next three generations are called Gen-X, Gen-Y and Gen Z. All of a sudden did they lose interest in naming the generation? I was unable to guess the reason.

Going through this classification, several questions arise. What exactly is the span of one generation? When and why does one end and the next one start? Why is the gap not uniform? There are different classifications, different dates, and different names given by different countries too.

I read recently that they have again changed the definition. There was a new generation every 15 years. Wow!!!! There is some sort of logic and maths here. This version says, Gen X are born between '65 to '80, Gen Y (or millennials) are those born between '80 to' 95, Gen Z are born between' 96 to 2010, and hold on. Then comes Gen alpha, those born after 2010. My head started reeling. Some people call Gen Z in our country as Zoomers or Zillenials. Lots of theories float by. I gave up my research.

I only roughly follow the nomenclature. I decided since I belong to the silent generation, I better be silent.

I feel as a senior I can be silent but not adamant and rigid like my joints. I have to change with the times, so that I am not considered a 'Neanderthal' by my grandchildren belonging to Gen Z. I may look old fashioned the way I dress up, but otherwise I should catch up a little with technological advancement, at least. The only way I can learn anything new happening in the outside world is by interacting with younger generations. For the Gen-Z, born after 1996 even the sky is not the limit of their imagination. They are dreaming of honeymooning on the Moon or settling down on Mars or exploring Jupiter and whatever.

Obviously they are not the cuddly toddlers anymore asking me for my silly bedtime stories. Actually the kids spin stories. One has published a book as a teenager and now continues writing scary stories of vampires, snakes, spirits etc. My grandson has created his own planet with dinosaur-like monsters and other exotic creatures. He has a blog and writes a lot. Another girl creates podcasts of her own. She gives valedictory addresses in the school etc. Given a chance she can talk on any subject. She and her sister are quite adept at playing games with X-boxes or recording iTunes. When they are interested in AI (artificial intelligence, which is far beyond my below par intelligence), coding on their laptops, writing apps, programming and blogging, they are on a different level altogether. When they plan a trip to the ISS or a space trip on board the 'Starship', their wavelength is far beyond my grasp and spectrum.

At the same time these grandchildren are so keen to know where they come from, what exactly their great, great, grandparents on both sides looked like, what they were, how they dressed up and where they lived etc. That is great and it is very important. But seriously when I am confronted with such questions, I fumble, mumble and stumble. To be honest, the lifespan of our grandparents was not much. My husband had not even seen his paternal grandfather. I was lucky to have seen both my grandfathers, but I hardly remember having any interaction with them.

Recently my granddaughter got her '23 and me' report done. This maps the 23 pairs of chromosomes in the human cell. It helps her to trace her ancestry and some relationships she is not aware of.

She wanted to analyse her DNA and so she got it mapped. She wants to go back in time a good 500 years or more uncovering her ethnic origins. She is so excited about the whole project. In fact she wanted us to get our DNA mapped too.

I told her. "Hey, even the priest who does the ceremony of our departed ancestors goes back only 3 generations".

"He might do that. But I want to go deep into the past. There is a trace of Central Asian, huge percentage of South Asian, a small percentage of North East, a good percentage of South Indian I have in my DNA. I want to know how it came to be," she said with determination. '23 and me' is perhaps the start of the game.

"Do you have photos of your grandparents?' my granddaughter asked. "Our Grandparents' pictures, yes, we have, of course," I told her. We had complete information about our parents and grandparents, a bit about our great grandfather, but beyond that we were shaky. She wanted to know more about them.

We have photographs of my husbands' grandparents and a grand uncle born 120 years back, perhaps around the time cameras were invented. Because it was a printed copy in black and white it survived all the handling and we could see it. I had scanned copies of sepia-tinted photographs of my great grandfathers, who perhaps departed 100 years back. One was that of a grand old man sitting cross legged, like a saint with sacred ash (Vibhuti) on his forehead, upper arms and chest. He has a string of 'Rudraksha' around his neck. He has a silvery beard and a stick in his hand indicating he was a sanyasi, a man who had renounced the world.

The other great grandfather's photo seems to have been taken in a studio. He is in his dhoti worn cross legged, and he has covered his upper body with an embroidered black shawl. Come to think of it, there are no photos of the grandmothers. I presume our grandmothers had no time to come out of the kitchen itself to pose for photos as they had huge families to take care of. Hey, 100 years back our ancestors were scared of being photographed because they believed taking photos would lessen their life span. Today's selfie sounds suicidal then!!

Imagine, these grandchildren of mine are 6 generations down the line. I wonder whether there is an alphabet generation-wise, to refer to our great, great, great, grandfathers. Can it be Gen-A?

Oh, yes, we both did know our great, great grandfathers and grand uncle's names and many of them were priests, astrologers and Vedic scholars. Some vague details I have are like they were 'Ayurvedic' doctors; one of them could even save victims of snake bites from death. There is a mysterious story connected to his death due to snakebite. The story goes that a cobra bit a young boy and it did not want him to be revived. But this old man took pity on the child and revived him by some magic spell and herbal concoctions. The cobra is said to have jumped from the tiled area in his courtyard that night, bit the old man and he died. Would today's children believe such stories? They would grill me with questions.

I told our grandchildren that one of my grand uncles was good at casting bronze icons and a few icons left with the descendants are being worshipped in their Pooja rooms. It seems that this grand uncle wanted to be an alchemist. It is said that one of the brothers of my grandfather was a budding mathematician who went to Varanasi, but unfortunately did not come back. What happened to him?

"Did he invent algebra?" asked one granddaughter eagerly. I laughed. Like this many questions remain unanswered and we can never get answers as all of them belong to the 'silenced forever generation'. Ultimately we found a family tree drawn by my father tracing unto 'his' great, great grandfather. But he himself could not get much information about their lives and lifestyles except that they lived in a tiny village called 'Orthanadu' near Thanjavur. In today's world perhaps we can even reach that great, great grandfather's ancestral home with the help of a google map if we only knew his address.

Similarly we have the family tree done by my brother-in-law, with all the ancestors' names written down but not much information about their profession, ancestral village and what ailment hit them and how old they were when they passed away.

Come to think of it, of what use are these photographs? When these grandchildren of ours see our childhood pictures, they are unable to believe we are the same people. The other day one of my cousins sent photos of my grandma's youthful appearance at 20 years of age on WhatsApp.

We all commented "oh, Patti looks so young and beautiful, and so different, almost 'unrecognisable".

Goodness, gracious, her own grandchildren, including me, have not recognised her!!!! For all that I am a grandma myself. Did I not know how old age digs its deep furrows on the face?

In the black and white pictures, I see my mother and aunts as brides or young mothers wearing antique jewellery, puff sleeves and ¾ sleeves, short sleeves, close necklines but never plunging necklines. They wear saris with wide borders in contrasting colours and a gorgeously designed 'pallu'. The chokers which are in fashion now are good old 'addigais'. The older generation had several holes bored in their ear lobes and around the edges and wore tiny little studs all around. They had jewels and rings on their noses. No rings around navel buttons and lips as is the fashion today.

Did I realise ever that my old aunts, uncles and grandparents were not born with dentures, or toothless mouths, thick bi-focal lenses, or replaced eye lenses, puffy eyes, drooping cheeks, double chin, rooster necks, silver hair, bald head and deep expression lines running down all over the face. We have a collection of family photos taken decades back on various occasions like weddings, sacred thread ceremonies, '60 th birthdays celebrations' called' 'Sashtiabdhapoorthi' celebrations. They are so precious. The grandchildren find such family photos in our old albums very interesting. We should hunt and get more of such old photographs. They will be with some very old people somewhere lying at the bottom of their steel trunks under their collection of handwritten letters, their wedding invitations about to break into pieces, and silk saris in a torn condition, obviously their wedding sarees

After all, nurturing relationships is good for our future. A family is the basic unit of a society and it is so wonderful to belong to a huge close-knit family.

They say 'Blood is thicker than water'.

Great grand Father of the Author.

29

I Was in a "Tearing" Hurry

It is good to listen to the unusual noises our body makes. As we grow old, the body does start protesting against its misuse, overuse and abuse in various ways. The protest may manifest quietly with fluids oozing out from some internal or external organ. It can be noisily protesting through any one of the orifices, as though crying for attention. I remember how my husband's ears used to be tuned to any little noise coming from any part of our old car. I wish he had heard my bones rubbing against each other or the meniscus or ACL tearing or ligament getting detached.

Until I was 70 I think, I did not have severe pain in the knee nor did I hear much cracking or tearing noise in my knees. I thought I escaped because I saw how much my elder sister was suffering from 'Arthritis' from the age of 50 or so. But I was wrong. The cartilage or ligament can tear at any age, the synovial fluid can dry up any time resulting in the rubbing of the bones calling for instantaneous 'cutting edges' technology.

Let's go back to noises the human body makes. For instance, snoring or burping. They are not life threatening, they are just annoying. Snoring, in the worst case scenario may end in a divorce and burping mostly subsides with a dose of antacid and a course of probiotics. But the worst is breaking wind aloud from the bottom rear end somewhat like the exhaust in the car. When it happens the person who breaks wind sitting in a group looks sheepishly around pretending to be unflustered or he/she may pull the chair, tap the sandals or cough noisily to drown the noise. It is highly embarrassing of course. The audience of this noisy performance either smile undercover or pretend to ignore.

Jokes apart, beware the crunchy noise, (only the person with the cracking knee can hear this noise) which announces the beginning of the injury to the knee. At the first sign of a popping noise at the knee joint, rush to the 'orthopaedic' surgeon. Unfortunately I did not.

Why did I turn a deaf ear to the noise my knees made? I don't know. Perhaps I thought creaking and buckling would stop. Slowly I gave up folding my legs or sitting on the ground. I avoided attending functions where I had to squat on the floor and eat on banana leaves. When climbing steps became painful, I gave up climbing. But that was no cure for my ailment. I was just avoiding the inevitable.

I was asked to go for walks to stop further deterioration of the joint by my children. But walking was quite unmanageable on broken pavements and moving between overflowing trash cans and barking stray dogs. On the road proper speeding cars missed me by an inch or two. Drivers 'started giving me advice, "Grandma, stay home, don't zig, zag on the road". In Madras language it was "veetle sollittu vanduttengala, (have you taken leave from your people back home)?".

It was then that I consulted an 'orthopedic' surgeon. He gave painkillers, glucosamine, and an extra dose of calcium tablets loaded with Vit. D3 of course. "You have to keep walking, you can't let the joint die," was the advice given by him. But the pain did not reduce and some friends suggested massage sessions at an 'Ayurveda Vaidya Sala' for a couple of weeks might help. Massages had to be continued for weeks together until the house started smelling like Vaidya Sala. It gave relief of course but it was temporary. At home bottles of oils filled the bedside table and tubes of desi, 'videsi' ointments found their place under my pillow.

Meanwhile an aunt of mine reported that she was happy with acupressure done by an expert. All I had to do was to press my fingertips and palms with my thumb and index finger. I put acute pressure on my husband to drive me 20 miles in Bangalore to see one such specialist. After some months I could bend my fingers better of course as I kept pressing the fingertips and the palms.

I decided to seriously postpone surgery as I was scared of the recovery. This was post floods when we shifted back to Bengaluru. The stage came when I could not get into a car and sit for long. At home I started having buffet dinners standing and walking around.

MRI, X-rays, and a battery of tests followed. One quick look the orthopedic surgeon took. He pronounced his verdict. "You have to go in for 'Total Knee Replacement' surgery. If you postpone anymore, you may end up in a wheelchair," he said. I could say nothing after that.

"Hey, have you not noticed that your friends, who used to sway from side to side, are able to walk straight now. They have their knee joints of titanium plates, my husband remarked. Women seem to be made for TKR or rather the plates are made for them.

'Sedentary lifestyle', mom. Don't argue that you homemakers do a lot of chores at home. That is not proper exercise. You should have gone for walks in the morning and evening. Now surgery seems the only option, said my children. Surgery at this age, no. What if it does not work!

How can I move with metallic or synthetic joints? The original joints made of bones, muscles, ligaments, patella, tendons and cartilages would be gone. Honestly I did not know the difference between any of these, but I just saw these names in the MRI report. But two metal plates moving like hinges on the doorframe might be tough to operate. I was reminded of the screeching noise our bathroom door made.

But all of a sudden, the day of surgery dawned. Before I could mentally get ready, I was there in the 'theatre'. "There is no general anaesthesia. It is only epidural; one injection in the spinal cord and the body waist down goes numb. You won't feel the pain", the surgeon reassured again with a smile. "For two weeks, we will give you strong medication for pain relief. Use ice packs liberally, you will recover with exercises within weeks, ('weeks' made it sound better than months)". Of course he wanted to boost my morale up.

I was there on the table surrounded by so many figures in white coats, caps, masks and gloves. I felt a prick or two in the back and slowly the numbness spread. The figures around became blurry.

'I am inside a huge mosquito net, what is it? I hear strange noises like hammering, sawing, clipping noises and some conversation in hushed tones also. The white figures kept going round and round. I am drowning somewhere.

When I opened my eyes with great effort I realized my tent and bright lights were gone. I was being rolled out. My body was bloating. My tummy was up somewhere. I was trying to press it down with my right hand, but my arm was dead. I felt bloated. Then again I was moving on a stretcher. I was back in my bed in the ICU. I could not breathe. Tubes pulled eew......it pained. I was sinking.

Was it the next day or the day after? But honestly I did not expect it to be so excruciatingly painful. A physiotherapist appeared from nowhere and said pain would go away with exercise. Three more days I was there in the ward being looked after very well by nurses and sisters. Injections, a 'palmful' of tablets and food were given in my bed. It was day 6, post-surgery; I was allowed to go home.

There are secrets which I want to tell the future TKR patients. Between you and me, "For a month or two post – surgery, bending the knee is tougher than bending Shiv Dhanush, which Rama broke to marry Sita". Sleeping in one posture, that is on your back for weeks together, you start feeling like an unlucky cockroach which turns turtle accidentally, keeps scratching the legs to roll over but cannot turn back to normal posture. I was not even as lucky as the cockroach since I could not even scratch my legs.

Cold ice packs in mid-winter gave relief. "A sort of numbness" was so comforting "Keep walking inside the house", said the doctor and the physiotherapist too, but with a walker. Ideally 120 degrees the leg has to bend. But at least 90 degrees while lying down or sitting", said the physiotherapist, who was helping me with my joints, he said I should cooperate. The very word 'operate' sounded ominous as I had just then undergone an operation.

"Now or never", was the mantra the therapist used every day meaning If I did not learn to bend within 4 to 6 weeks, I would never do it. Scary indeed. The surgeon had already accomplished successfully what he had to do. The X-ray showed the plates sitting neatly. The rest of my recovery rested with me. Like a toddler taking her first steps, I learnt how to walk, that too with a walker. As a toddler I used my siblings as walkers I am sure.

I had to stretch the hamstring, strengthen the quadriceps, and extend the calf muscle. "Start with pumps, even 100 times a day is fine. Two things you should remember, don't twist the knee and don't fall", was the advice given by the surgeon when I was discharged.

These few verbs I heard in my daily conversation. They were pump, press, tighten, stretch, bend, and fold. It was like the priest's 'swaha' while pouring ghee in the fire while doing a 'homam'. But had he not insisted I might not have walked like I walk today. Well, I am on the road to recovery. I even got titanium plates replacing my natural joint in the other leg. Hurray!!! Hats off to the surgeons who do such marvels with their nimble fingers cutting through skin, bones, muscles, ligaments and cartilages sawing the bones, fixing and sticking the plates, and stapling the rest of them neatly. He does it all up within an hour or two. Most of us can't join two frayed edges of a cloth straight; imagine stitching up human skin, flesh, and the loosely hanging fibres. Awesome!!!

30

Covid Era

Please let me write about the city and the colony I live in, at Bengaluru. Our colony is a huge gated complex with good security, green environment, clean roads and all other facilities. The construction is solid as the main walls are built of granite. When it came up initially 32 years back it seemed to be in the outskirts of the city in quiet surroundings with nothing urban about it. There was a small shopping centre, a post office, a bank, a park and a nursery school. Most of the permanent residents of our society were retired service personnel hailing from different regions of the country. They were leading leisurely post-retirement lives browsing the newspapers in the mornings and going for walks in the evening.

But by the turn of the century, our colony became a much sought-after apartment complex as Bengaluru became the Silicon Valley of India. As the name changed, policies changed, economic conditions changed and too many MNCs started operating from here, changing the old garden city into an IT hub. From a cool, calm, clean city, Bengaluru was turning into a busy, bustling, and bursting-at-its's-seams city. It had to accommodate the swelling migrant population requiring housing, water, roads and electricity. The pensioner's paradise was becoming a heaven for upwardly mobile youth from all corners of India and the pensioners lost their paradise. Sorry, I am not writing my own "Paradise Lost" here. Millions of computer qualified youngsters chose to make Bangalore their home and the city extended in all directions though it was not ready for the huge expansion infrastructure-wise.

We were back at Bengaluru by the end of the year 2016 after a break of 16 years and the deluge in Chennai. I have described it in the previous chapter perhaps more elaborately than required. That was our loss.

It took some time for us to settle down back in Bengaluru. Anyway time and tide wait for nobody's connections and change of address or whatever. Months rolled on irrespective of our changes.

It was the month of Feb '20. We saw the breaking news on the TV channel one morning that an Indian girl, a medical student, who had come from Wuhan, China, was diagnosed with Covid.19-Sars-2. She was the first case as such diagnosed and treated in a hospital in Kerala. She had brought it straight from the oven, I mean, Wuhan, the birthplace of the virus. The exact source still remained a mystery.

Our country was very far from Wuhan, China. Well, that is what we all thought. But how it spread from one case in Kerala in the month of January to several hundreds within two months across India sent shock waves besides the virus waves. It seemed to be deadly dangerous as it killed many of the victims. Soon it was wreaking havoc not only in India but in 114 countries around the world killing millions in its wake. It was then announced as a PANDEMIC at last, as scary as the Spanish flu a 100 years back or Bubonic plague nearly 700 years back.

The PM of our country announced his decision at 8pm, on 23rd. March, 2020, to impose a complete national lock-down from midnight that very day. The entire nation was shocked, (though most of them later agreed that was perhaps the only way to go). People who were out of their homes had to freeze wherever they were as the buses, trains and airlines stopped their services at midnight. Lakhs of migrant workers started running away (literally) scared of being jobless, homeless and moneyless. That created a terrible situation because they were carrying home the deadly virus to spread it even in their remote villages. By the time the authorities-in-charge reacted the workers had left for their homes and those who lived in the outskirts of the cities reached home too by then. A lot of them suffered walking miles at a stretch and some lost their lives, it was a terrible situation.

The next morning, March 24th, we felt the impact of the lockdown in our own apartment complex. The overcast sky, the deserted roads, the carpet of dry leaves, and the gray granite walls of the apartments with the windows 'shut tight' deepened the gloomy atmosphere. An eerie silence descended on the entire neighbourhood. That was day 1 of the lockdown 1.0. Everywhere the topic discussed was Covid, Covid, Covid and nothing else.

"Build up immunity with vit. C, D 3, and zinc," said the doctors. They were being interviewed on TV. The pharmacies had a sudden shortage of those tablets. "Ayurvedic" herbs and herbal concoctions can prevent and control the disease better," said the Ayurvedic practitioners. Neem, ginger, garlic, lemons, turmeric, pepper, honey and herbal powders were in great demand. Hence the prices of these items shot up. Elderly people started inhaling steam every hour. Tea in all shades was drunk in gallons provided there was someone to make them.

Lockdown naturally meant no movement on the roads and no domestic help could enter our gated complex. Back in our house dirty dishes and unwashed, unfolded clothes piled up for 48 hours. Dusty furniture, un-swept floors, grimy kitchen counters, ugh.. presented a depressing picture. For 54 years my husband has not stood by me, I mean in the kitchen, now after a week of lockdown, he was there with me. As he could not stand the house being dirty. He started helping me out with the chores. We rang the bells, clapped hands, and stood with lamps lit to show our gratitude to our doctors and healthcare workers. We had to drive the virus away, come what may.

Lockdown 2.0, 3.0, 4.0 followed. Working men and women were asked to work from home. WFH became the order of the day. Zoom meetings, google meet, conference calls, call them whatever, became the order of the day for working couples almost 24x7. Some people could see at times the elder family members hovering in the background giving a helping hand, thankfully not with the official calls, but supplying lunch, snacks, tea or coffee.

Women 'Working from Home' were hit harder as usual. They had to manage mischievous toddlers in tantrums or tiny infants demanding attention. The three year olds had to be trained to sit with computers turning living rooms into play schools. We could hear the 'hungama' around in zoom meetings and online classes at times.

We added quite a lot of new words to our vocabulary. First of all the word Corona was even on a toddler's lips and lisps. It was only known to virologists earlier (in Wuhan, where it originated) and others of their ilk in the outside world. Comorbidities, a morbid term which most of us seniors were unaware of, became a word we were scared of. Later we realised that they were the same as 'pre-existing conditions' of the insurance that we took when we visited our children abroad. The word 'morbid' sounded so 'horrid'. Loss of smell was 'anosmia 'and loss of taste was 'dysgeusia'. 'Covid appropriate behaviour' and 'Covid protocol' were the new rules to be followed. 'Quarantining' and 'social distancing' made us feel miserable and isolated. We are social animals after all. We Indians were thrilled that 'Namaste' was chosen as the best form of greeting even on alien shores as it went up in popularity charts.

Senior citizens were happy with a rerun of all mythological TV serials ever produced being shown on TV and kids were delighted with their Chota Bheem, 'Bada Man' Spider-Man, Superman, Shaktimaan etc. on television, though we realised 'no man' was superior to a tiny virus even.

Doctors were in huge demand not only professionally but for interviews on TV channels 24 x 7. They were the saviours. They advised repeatedly never to touch the nose and mouth after wearing a mask. Not touching the mouth and nose was a bit 'asking too much' for Indians, who are used to chewing, scratching, spitting and picking their noses in public. Hence they hated masks, which would block all their facial orifices; most of them avoided wearing them.

The deadly virus was spreading fast and infected millions. None in the family were allowed to visit their loved ones if they were hospitalised. They were in the ICU and all of a sudden they vanished. That was an extremely tragic situation. We felt the pain when we lost dear friends and relatives in this manner. Quite a few young cousins passed away helplessly as neither the prevention nor the cure was available.

The war veterans of our colony had never faced such a formidable enemy in any aggression on our soil. They had won various medals, awards and honours for their meritorious service to the nation. They had won the Bangladesh war and the 'Kargil' war. Of course Corona virus was more like an infiltrator, a 'hard-core' terrorist, hitting the humans' right in the core of their lungs. This terrorist was invisible and invincible too by surgical strikes or bombing of their hideouts. There was no strategy to prevent him or counter him at the entry point. Several variants started appearing in different countries. The world of researchers was focusing on finding a vaccine.

It almost seemed to be a mission impossible. But after one year of research in many countries around the world, several vaccines came out to help humanity against the attack of Coronavirus. By 15th of Jan '2021 our country could offer two vaccines, one was 'Covishield' and the other was 'Covaxin'. The latter was completely indigenous. The vaccination drive started with doctors, nurses and other frontline workers in hospitals and people in the police force, fire services, paramedics, and ambulance drivers. Senior citizens got their turn next as they were more vulnerable to 'comorbidities' and many lost their lives. When life started to come back to some sort of normalcy, another variant started attacking the young and middle aged even. Lakhs of people fell victim to the Delta variant of Covid-19 in the summer of 2021. The country lost precious doctors, nurses, and other frontline warriors and thousands of others. Any number of beds, ventilators and oxygen cylinders seemed not enough and the death toll of victims kept going up.

It was at this time I lost my only sister. Even when she was bedridden (not due to Covid), we could not go because the world did not know how to treat the patient hit by the virus. We were advised against travelling. We could not cross from state to state.

The variants moved around donning Greek alphabetical names though the disease was from yet another country. But slowly the vaccination, especially if both shots were taken, seemed to reduce the spread but a booster shot became necessary too. The unpredictable behaviour of the variants is still shrouded in mystery.

"To stay safe and avoid Covid-19, the best and the only way is to wear a mask," was and is the advice given by every doctor, researcher, actor, cricketer, minister and even a friendly next door neighbour and in all the TV channels and newspapers. Some people thought covering the mouth was good enough; closing the nose was asking a bit too much. Some covered their chin with the mask just in case...the police appeared, they could quickly pull it up. They were more worried about the police imposing the fine. Some kept the mask very stylishly on top of their head.

Enough demos had been given on TV by celebrities wearing beautiful masks of course, obviously gifts from the sponsors. Coming to masking the face looks did not seem to matter anymore. Masks had made it unnecessary to use face cream, powder, lipstick, or any makeup. A man could go out with an unshaven face and a scraggly beard. In short, human faces were not recognizable anymore. People just walked on ignoring their own friends.

Choosing and managing a mask seemed quite a task. For some the mask kept slipping down the nose. Masks with two elastic bands and spectacles were not a convenient combo. But it was a question of living with both spectacles and mask or leave the world without both.

Our celebrities found a way to make the mandatory mask into a fashion statement. The film stars carried it with such style and 'elan, Hey, soon the market was flooded with designer masks and masks in all colours. Hats off, I mean masks off, to you fashionistas for setting the trend.

There was some hope for mankind. All was not lost and we gained a 'mask' as an additional accessary to our attire.

31

Virtual Wedding in Covid Era

Families which had planned weddings of their children were caught in a tight corner during 'Covid' era. The idea of 'big fat weddings', 'thematic weddings', and 'destination weddings,' had to be given up completely. Many of them postponed their weddings by a month or two thinking the virus would somehow disappear. But after almost a year there was no sign of the epidemic receding though research was going on in several countries.

But, man, sorry, woman too, always finds a way out of difficult situations. One matrimonial website suggested it could organise virtual weddings in COVID-19 times:

"That is the way to go," said many young couples. A virtual wedding which the guests could see over 'Zoom' became the trend of Covid era. We had one such wedding in our close family circle and the venue was Washington D.C. it was going to be 'Washingtonil Virtual Tirumanam'. My peer group will recall the popular hilarious story published in a popular Tamil weekly 'titled 'Washingtonil Tirumanam' way back...when I was a teenager.

Even the grandparents of the bride could not attend. Cousins in dozens were itching to take domestic flights in the US to reach Washington but it was too risky for anyone to fly in a crowded aircraft. Everyone could visualise the deadly Coronavirus hanging inside droplets or in aerosols in the air in airports and inside the aircrafts. Road trips would involve trips to the rest rooms en-route, which sent shivers down every spine as they visualised the virus getting into their nostrils.

It was decided that the virtual wedding would be watched by a hundred close relatives and friends at least, living not only in the USA but all around the world, on their desktop, laptop, iPad or even smart phones, over a 'Zoom' call. We all got ready in the comfort of our homes. We were in various time zones and we were engaged in different activities depending on our own wall clocks and biological clocks. We were told some were sipping coffee in San Francisco; some lucky ones were dipping their 'idlis' in Sambar in Houston, or biting a salty toast. While a fortunate few in London had their 'aloo paratha' with pickles on their plate and cups of yoghurt by the side and many of us in India had finished our dinner even, as it was 8 pm.

Virtual or real, a wedding is a wedding, a joyous occasion to celebrate. So we women dressed up in colourful silk saris and some light jewellery as on zoom they generally show the guests once or twice. We could not present ourselves in a nightdress as it was past dinner. In fact, we looked made up and ready for a family photo. Hey, that should be the next invention to pick up the people from various continents, blend them like a collage and make a family photo. That would be great!!!!

The bride entered the scene looking radiant in a grand white 'Banarasi' sari with a dazzling red border and a gorgeous 'pallu'. She had glittering gold jewellery on and had flowers (which looked fresh) in her freshly washed hair. The groom was looking tall and handsome in a silken 'Sherwani' suit. The place was decked up with flowers and lamps (electric of course). The bride's parents, a younger brother and the groom's sister were following the purohit's instructions. The Purohit (sastrigal) was in Chicago on the same Zoom call and mantras he chanted were live-streamed.

Could anyone have imagined this sort of technology taking over conducting rituals, even a few years back! Incredible! The Purohit, the bridal couple and the invitees, were all connected by Wi-Fi and they could see each other and talk to each other. Is it not a marvel?

Desperate calls for joining the zoom meet started.

'I am unable to join, hold on', a grand aunt was announcing in an excited voice.

"I am not getting the image," said an uncle with a sad face.

"Oh, God, my microphone is not switching on", complained another.

"My name is not there in the list," said another invisible voice.

"I can't hear the mantra, where is the sastry", interrupted another grand aunt.

These were the phone calls from grand uncles and grand aunts to each other, who were struggling to get onto the zoom call. For old timers like us, it is tough to keep up with technology. But we do not want to miss out on anything. These are small hiccups. It is more the user's lack of expertise than the failure of technology.

"Well, well, the Sastrigal is conducting the wedding from Chicago. Obviously you cannot see him, but you can hear him. He sounds like an oracle. That is all", a tech-savvy aunt explained.

She was thrilled as she could watch the proceedings, hears the mantras and had her name and image on the list. The sastrigal must be a veteran in performing virtual weddings. It is at this juncture we zoom into the call.

The boy at this stage declares he is going to Kashi (Varanasi). The father-in-law requests him to kindly come back and marry his daughter. The brother-in-law brings an umbrella and other paraphernalia and takes him in. The bride welcomes him with a garland. They exchange garlands three times. This is called Kashi 'Yatra'. They could neither go out nor come in. Remember it was Covid era and they were in Washington, DC. But the mantras were not given a miss.

In India there is a lot of fun and frolic around this custom. Uncles would carry their nieces and nephews higher and higher on their shoulders so garlanding gets tougher and tougher. Uncles and the crowd enjoy it immensely. But in the zoom meet it was not possible.

A word about the garlands. Due to the pandemic, fresh flowers were avoided. Bride's mom made matching red and white satin rose garlands for the girl and the boy respectively, sanitised, sprayed with perfume. Next ritual was holding a silk dhoti in between the boy and the girl and when it was lifted the bride and groom were supposed to see each other for the first time. This was a tradition being followed for more than a hundred years in our country when the boy and the girl, maybe, actually saw each other for the first time, but it is a tradition we follow till now.

Zoom back to Washington. Sastrigal wanted the couple to pour cups of yellow rice on each other's heads. Mom carefully brought some manageable quantity as it is tough to sweep and mop the wooden floor of the brand new apartment after the event. Next is the tying of 'Mangalyam'. Sister-in-law (the groom's sister) was standing ready to do her bit of tying the third knot to confirm and reconfirm the bond.

Next, Sastrigal, asked the bride's father to place the aluminium foil 'homa kundam' and start the fire with a starter kit, a few twigs (called samiti) and spoonfuls of ghee. The bride's brother had a handful of puffed rice to be offered in the fire. He had to constantly keep an eye on the smoke alarm a few feet away on the ceiling. He was standing guard right below the alarm till that minute. If the alarm started blaring, it would be a situation to face. Unfortunately, it had no batteries to remove. Otherwise, I remember how the battery was removed from the smoke alarm once when we had to make hot 'Bhajjis' for my grandson's birthday party. He insisted on having only onion 'bajjis' as his birthday gift.

Coming back to the wedding, the couple took their circumambulations, the 'saat phere' around the sacred fire with the groom's shawl, and the bride's sari tied in a knot.

Next step was to take the mandatory 'Saptapadis'. While the groom holds his wife's foot the bride takes the steps one by one and they take their 7 vows. The wedding ceremony as such was complete. The Purohit wanted 'Ammi (the flat grinding stone of yore, which even homemakers in India have got rid of) to be kept for the bride to put her foot on and promptly a small round stone was placed and the bride placed her foot on it. The toe rings were gently slipped in her second toe by the boy. Fast forward to star gazing, I mean the bride taking a look at Arundhati. They looked through the window at the blue sky and the boy pointed out the star in the vast firmament. He was telling her to be an exemplary wife like the 'rishi patni'. Hindu traditions and rituals are highly symbolic and we have strong faith that these will stand the couple in good stead.

Then the Sastrigal conducted ''nalangu', a little fun with a golden ring thrown in a small pot of water. The couple had to put their hands and pick up the ring, each trying to grab the ring but grab each other's fingers instead. The winner felt triumphant as he became lord of the ring,' Aarti was to be taken as the rituals were coming to an end. The bride's mom sang 'Sitakalyana vaibhogame' in a very sweet voice. Sastrigal did not omit any tradition or custom. It was perfect.

Congratulatory messages from grandparents, elders who were seated in their homes were shown. Everyone was beaming and felt very happy that the wedding went off beautifully and they could watch the whole ritual. They missed it in flesh and blood but the spirit and the essence of it they saw. Blessings and best wishes poured in. The couple looked blissfully happy.

We all witnessed the wedding and we had a great time with the unique experience of watching a virtual wedding wherein we could meet our relatives whom we had not seen for a long time. We were back on our beds in a couple of hours. No travel, no hassles, no exposure to Corona, and yet we saw and were a part of all the proceedings at a venue far away from us.

What else could you ask for in 2020 while the pandemic was raging in the USA and in the whole world?

We heard of such virtual weddings taking place in our own country. The best part here was the hosts organised to send a grand wedding feast packed in a tiffin carrier kept inside a beautiful basket to each and every invitee at lunch time. That was a typical example of our tradition 'atithi devo bhava'. How we could quickly 'Indianise' the whole event in such an innovative manner.

Wow, is that not the way to go!!!

32

Astro Apps Are In

Astrology along with astronomy has been known to mankind for thousands of years. Astronomers and mathematicians from ancient civilizations like Mesopotamia, China, Greece and India were convinced that the stars and planets in the sky had an unfathomable link and an incomprehensible influence on the lives of mankind on earth. In short they sought to provide a connection between man/woman and the cosmos, in other words between microcosm and macrocosm.

The Hindu astronomers learnt how to cast an almanac or calendar more than three thousand years back around 1200 BCE or even earlier. When they cast the almanac initially they based their calculations on the cycles of the moon. The majority of Indians follow the luni-solar calendar and for them the New Year starts in the middle of March. For those who follow the solar calendar the New Year starts on the 14th of April. But for all practical purposes and to follow a standard calendar worldwide people follow the Gregorian calendar, which again is a solar calendar. As a result someone made an APP for the computer with the help of which a horoscope can be cast given the date, time and place of birth of the baby.

Otherwise in India an astrologer casts a baby's horoscope when he is given similar details about the place of his/her place of birth, the day, the date according to the Hindu almanac or Gregorian calendar and exact time up to the second of the birth of the baby. The Hindu almanac has the details regarding the presiding star at that particular second in the firmament and the phase of the moon on that day. The position of the sun, moon, and the nine planets in the zodiac is noted down. In days of yore, the learned scholars, who had studied astronomy, astrology and mathematics, were the men who cast the horoscopes. They were consulted for casting the horoscope and forecasting the life of the newborn too. They could foretell the personal characteristics and attributes of the child and what sort of life in general he/she could expect to live through.

In our country, there are millions who have absolute faith in astrology, and take their major and minor decisions after consulting their own family astrologers. There are many, including politicians, who in fact believe in god-men who are all-knowing and hence advise them on various matters. Besides money, marriage and business ventures, they perhaps give advice on all decisions they make regarding their political moves. And there are those who call themselves rationalists and atheists who do not believe in astrology and the predictions. In between there are those who call themselves agnostics who neither believe nor disbelieve. When confronted by old age, disease, accident, death of a dear one or sudden downfall in fortunes and failures in any venture, men and women start looking to the heavens. Of course for the young their education, career, marriage, or sudden health problem makes them seek some guidance to direct them in the right path for finding a solution When a person is in a very weak and vulnerable situation every human wants some reassurance. It is at this juncture perhaps astrologers come into picture for many of them.

As far as I remember my parents only consulted an astrologer when the time came for their children to get married. Especially when the girl in the family crossed the age of 18, 20 or so it used to be a serious topic between elders. “Have you taken out her horoscope? Make copies,” “You should start looking for a good alliance for your daughter, it takes years sometimes, “such suggestions would pour in from curious outsiders too. For ages marriages in our country have been ‘arranged marriages’, in which the parents plan the alliance taking into consideration many factors. The game generally starts with the exchange of horoscopes and then goes through several stages. Both the parents try to find out about the family background, their status and standing in the society, their views and ideas on many things before giving or taking the horoscope from them.

To begin with, it is the ‘gotra’ which could be the first hurdle.

If the boy and the girl belonged to the same ‘gotra’, which indicated the ‘rishi’ (the saintly ancestor) from whom their family descended, it would mean they belonged to the same lineage. In this case the boy and the girl were like siblings and hence they could not marry each other. Many proposals would get dropped at this earliest stage like a ton of bricks.

The next hurdle could be the birth star of the girl and the boy. This had to match. According to believers in astrology there are good stars and there are ‘not-so-good stars and there are very bad stars. The astrologer could declare a particular star not good for the would-be-mother-in-law and another star might not portend well for the father-in-law. There are stars which are just not good for the boy and the girl to get married to each other. They could go for other alliances of course. The position of planet Mars at the time of birth of the person played a major role. For example, for the girl if it was in the wrong 'house 'it was a blemish or fault ('kalatra dosham'), it was not good for the spouse. In that case the boy should have the same 'dosham', (literally means' a blemish'). If the horoscopes matched the groom would come to see the girl. Ugh......otherwise the proposal would end then and there.

To come to that stage of 'boy coming to see the girl' was a long journey those days. Ultimately the 'bachelor boy' would step into the girl's house with his entire brood to 'see her' and to enjoy 'the bajjis' and 'sooji halwa' made in honour of his visit. Invariably the girl would be asked to sing on that occasion. Many times it would be the first and the last such request for her performance. If the girl came out successful after this stage, the boy's party would declare after a lot of deliberation and 'thinking' that it is a 'yes' from them. Some parents would put the blame entirely on the stars and gods that marriages are made in heaven and it was not in their hands or some such excuse.

That brings me to the latest I read about astrological predictions. The reports say that millennials at least 75 % of them believe in astrology today. They are said to show a lot of interest in the 'astro apps' available on the Internet. Next to Whatsapp this 'astro app' is said to be of great interest to them. It is called the mystical 'services market,' in their stressful lives and lifestyles they perhaps find comfort in such predictions. If they are good, they are happy. I think perhaps it is a 'time pass' for some youngsters. Or they have faith and it might help them to make decisions on the job front, promotions, changing the job etc. It might help them to identify their friends or foes in the workplace etc.

I always wondered why the media, the print as well as the electronic one carry daily, weekly or monthly forecasts till I came to know about the millennials' newfound love for astrology.

Little wonder then that the day's predictions on the TV channels seem very popular. There must be a huge viewership and the TRS rating must be high too.

Millions of people fall under twelve zodiac signs depending on their dates of birth according to the Gregorian calendar or the stars under which they are born according to Hindu calendar. That means that day should be the same luck-wise or otherwise for people born under the same sign. Wow.

No wonder then that tarot readers and astrologers are in great demand not only in India but on alien shores too. Numerology became popular sometime back when celebrities started adding extra 'a's and's's. When it comes to dating or making decisions regarding love affairs, today's youngsters are said to depend on the zodiac signs. The age group is said to be anywhere between 15 to 30. Amazing!

Leave alone the media forecasts, even today we come across the 'kili josyars,' and a small crowd standing in front of him watching the fun or consulting him. The astrologer sits with a parrot in a cage. He has a set of cards spread on a sheet in front. The minute a question is asked, the payment is made, the parrot is out, picks up a card and someone makes a major decision depending on the card the parrot picks. It is somewhat similar to a tarot card reading, I presume.

Palmistry is also said to be a science. In a social gathering, if someone says he knows a little bit of palmistry, one should see the number of hands stretched in front of him both left and right, the former for men and the latter for women. Someone would like to know how strong his career line is. Another likes to know about his heart line and one would love to know the length of his life.

The questions the young ones generally ask are said to revolve around love marriage and whether they have fallen in love with the right person or not. Some astrologers perhaps promise that they can do some adjustments, remedial measures can be found if the boy is very serious about the affair. 'Jyotishis' are a powerful lot and the youth are vulnerable and emotional. When couples fight, engagements get broken, marriages get postponed indefinitely, and businesses seem to be not picking up, the young or old get upset and depressed. Anxiety, ambition and depression among the youth are said to be rampant. High schoolers are anxious about their entrance tests, college admissions and careers. On the whole the astrologers are now approached by more youngsters.

Around 350 apps on astrology are said to be available on the internet. Google search is going up day by day. Well then, we can say "astrology is here to stay".

33

Shopping through the Decades

Once my husband retired from active service I felt very old. I started introspecting and going mentally through my childhood. How as the youngest child I had a lovely time with no work and all play. Many factors go into making a happy childhood. I think lots of siblings, friends, playing outdoor games, lots of outings and lots of festivals to celebrate and sweets and snacks to eat and fun during mealtimes can make a happy childhood. But I cannot forget the shop that was there on our street corner. I see it in my dreams sometimes. It was diagonally opposite to our house but the wonder was if my mother called from the window of our kitchen, the shopkeeper could hear her and he would ask her from the door of his shop what she wanted. He had a million things in his small shop. He sold grocery items besides biscuits, chocolates, and many types of hard candies displayed in huge glass bottles kept on top of his cabinet. There were lollipops, lemon drops, jeera peppermints in pink and white (called 'arisi' peppermint), the black and white striped hard candy, strong peppermints in pink and white, fig centred candy ......by the way, why is it not made anymore?

"It used to be so good; it used to be so nice,

Whatever happened to that candy, I wish I understood," as ABBA's lyrics are in a popular song. We could get a bar of Cadbury's chocolate for 25 paise or 'naalana'. A 100gms of fresh 'nendran banana chips' we could buy for the same price, 100gms of salted cashew nuts cost a rupee or maybe less. Can you believe that all these yummies were sold just across the road? Any visiting uncle or aunt would give me a rupee as a parting gift and the next minute I would rush and buy a bar of chocolate, chips and fig-centre candy too.

My mother would be making 'dosa' and she would realise that she did not have fried gram to make chutney. I would run and buy it. The salesman would weigh the fried gram and pour it so efficiently in a paper cone made by rolling a piece of newspaper then and there. With great expertise he would fold and tuck the top ends rolling the cone in a circular fashion and tie it up with a piece of thin jute string pulled from a huge ball of jute thread hanging above his head with the greatest expertise all within 2 or 3 minutes. He deserved a WOW really. In the past no one went shopping without cloth bags. Actually the bags were used till their seams tore or they became too grimy and the passers-by moved away from it. No carry bags were ever given. Newspaper or brown paper packets and jute thread, the shop keepers used were biodegradable too. All grocery shops did the same type of packing whether it was 100gms or even 1 kilo. By the way the weights and measurements were very different then unlike the metric system in use now. Oh, no, it is too much to explain. I am not going there.

I presume by the 60'sand 70's shopping became more complicated as our needs increased because of lifestyle changes. The products were much more in variety than earlier. But our corner shop was there selling all the commodities, perhaps at a slightly higher price, but not too expensive, because inflation was not much those days. In some countries such shops are called 'convenience stores'. But the saddest thing was we had moved out from that corner house and there was no corner shop or convenience store for us from then on.

I got married and I shifted to New Delhi to set up my home by the mid-sixties. Quite often we went to Janata Bazaar there. It was said that Janata bazaar introduced a new concept in shopping One could shop for groceries, utensils, garments, toiletries, home appliances and plastics under one roof. One could buy tins, bins, baskets, brooms, bottles, brushes, cleaning liquids, curtains and just about anything for setting up a house. On the whole, Janata Bazaar was an interesting place to shop as it was spread out in 2 or 3 floors.

By the 70's and 80's many new developments took place. A wide range of household appliances like refrigerators, wet grinders, mixies, bread toasters, and baking ovens appeared in the market. Sure enough they entered middle class homes though at a slower pace. Since they were made in India, they were affordable. Earlier women in Madras went to buy 'Moulinex' or 'Braun' mixie in a shop in George Town.

These gadgets made a lot of difference to the lifestyles of the middle class population. Along with the refrigerators came the desire to make ice creams. Women started making ice creams and puddings at home with milk, food colours, essence, stabilisers etc. puddings were made at home with custard powder, gelatine and jellies in the fridge. The fridge made it all possible. The ingredients had to be bought. Hmmm..... Homemakers loved to bake cakes and cookies too. There were several enterprising women who started classes to make jams, squashes and juices also. Homemakers had become overactive. And there were others who taught baking and cooking. My sister started teaching baking and she authored and published books on how to make cakes and cookies at home. Cookery books in English and other regional languages started getting published. Women's magazines had two or three pages at least filled with recipes of sorts. Housewives bought a baking oven too. Naturally it made the shopping list long, much longer than before.

In the next ten years huge departmental stores selling more items including small home appliances, gift items, crockery, fancy things made of plastic spread over a vast area became popular as shopping under one roof was found to be convenient. People required such retail shops which not only stacked every essential item under one roof but they were displayed nicely and the customer could go around picking the items in the baskets or a trolley provided by the shop. Pushing the trolley to the cash counter and paying up the bill made shopping a pleasure. Eventually such retailers started their shops in several cities and they formed a chain of stores.

But our old corner shops known as 'Kirana' up north remained in the same spots for years in every neighbourhood. Such convenience stores were always popular in our country because of their proximity, reasonable prices of the commodities, faster attention to the customers, and flexibility in payments as regular neighbourhood customers could even make monthly payments.

The Tupperware entered with a lot of fanfare. They were sold at exclusive parties and stored in special warehouses. The elite of the society stored Oil dripper to 'idly' batter in expensive Tupperware containers. Tupperware was the talk of urban housewives. It was the new craze.

Around the 80's a revolution in marketing technique took place. Thanks to a man living in a small town in Tamilnadu. He got a brilliant idea. The concept struck him out of the blue when he was looking at a boy with unkempt hair. He wondered why a shampoo used by the rich to wash their hair cannot be used by the poor. Why can't it be made affordable and accessible to him? Lo, behold, a sachet was born. He tried an experiment in his own factory. He succeeded in making a sachetand filled it with a small quantity of a liquid and a sachet of 'velvet' shampoo was born. The rest is history. Next came the hair oils, honey, detergents, instant coffee and betel nuts and scores of other products.

The sachets were sold in millions. Yes, the sachet was just one time use. But they were cheap and buyable. While a fancy bottle of shampoo cost a hundred rupees or more this sachet was Rs. 2. Daily wage earners who frequented the neighbourhood corner shops could buy the sachets without hesitation. A poor mother could satisfy the desire of her 4 year old by buying a packet of potato chips, popcorn, 'Kurkure' for him to munch. The youth were aware of good grooming, makeup and looking handsome. Credit goes to the popular TV commercials. Any cosmetic was in great demand. It became a win-win situation both for the sellers and the buyers. Colourful sachets were hung like curtains right at the entrance of corner shops and grocery shops. They sold sachets in millions.

The world of business was changing fast. Brand name became very important. Advertising and publicity played very big roles.

Showrooms, huge retail shops, outlet shops, malls became very popular. Today's shopping scenario is entirely different. Buying things on credit cards has increased considerably. People started buying on the spur of the moment as they were not paying then and there; it gave them a sort of freedom to buy more and more. There is so much competition and the advertisements by way of huge posters, hoardings, full page ads in dailies and commercials on television do wonders to the businesses. Celebrities especially from the world of cinema, cricket, and other sports started doing endorsements. Young men and women joined business schools to master the art of administration, accounting, and advertising, strategy of selling and building up big businesses.

The 'pettikadai' (the tiny corner shop) is still there and his customers remain the same, those who stay in the neighbourhood and keep a monthly account, which also is perhaps a sort of credit card.

The malls attract lots of people, perhaps for browsing or as "timepass' or as a meeting place for friends more than shopping seriously. The mall culture has caught on here in our country like the rest of the world.

Oh, yes, how can I forget shopping online, the latest convenient shopping for senior citizens? Online shopping especially for essential grocery items and vegetables etc. was found to be a boon during Covid Era. Now the practice continues. Except that we had to give up shopping completely even for garments, footwear and other necessities, which gave us a lot of choice and a chance to go out. Online shopping is the latest luxury of 21st century. Amazon, Big Basket, Flip cart and several others have found millions of regular customers online.

I am sure some other new trend is waiting round the corner to appear and attack us. In today's world, novelty sells.

Sachet Curtain

34

It is Never too Late for Yoga

I remember my aunt who visited us years back in Hyderabad. We had moved to that city on posting only a few weeks earlier. My aunt was a yoga expert, who started practicing yoga from a very young age. She believed in meditation too. I could see she was looking very young and energetic. We were meeting after a long break. She was prepared to teach me yoga 'asanas' and Pranayama. She was prepared to stay with us for a couple of days for that purpose. But I did not learn.

"She smiled and said," you can find time if you want to". "Where will I find time for deep breathing and holding my breath? I don't seem to find time for ordinary breathing," I replied with a smile too. I was always fond of finding excuses for postponing any physical exercise. I could have found time if I was really keen on learning. She was right. She lived in the same city. I could have gone to her house even, (which was not quite close though. See another excuse"). Anyway I missed that great opportunity.

Another aunt and her whole family were and are still yoga enthusiasts. She too tried to tell me that yoga was the answer for all my vague pains and aches. When she passed away, she was 94. She could do such tough exercises like pushing a thread through one nostril and pulling it out from the other nostril. This was called 'sutra Neti', she told me. She poured water through one nostril and brought it out from the mouth. This maneuver looked so complicated. It was called 'Jal Neti', she explained. Wow, quite a trick it was. I felt she was performing it like a magician. Perhaps at that time when she demonstrated these, she had crossed 75 years of age. It was amazing.

My uncle was another yoga buff. His hip joint got disjointed; I mean the ball came out of the socket in the hip in a road accident. It remained disconnected for some hours as he could not reach a hospital for several hours after the accident. The next day, the surgeon put the ball into the socket alright but that was that. The surgeon felt that it may not come back to normal as the tissues had died in that 20 hour delay. He warned my uncle that he may have to prepare himself to spend the rest of his life in a wheelchair. But there he was, I mean my uncle who went back to doing his rigorous Hatha yoga exercises. He almost regained his walking with a slight limp. He could walk with a stick and did not restrict himself to wheeling around the house ever till he died at a ripe old age of 93. Was it his sheer will power that kept his joint alive?

Another aunt was an Ayurveda fan. I am talking about what happened a long time ago, maybe, more than 60 years back. She used to advocate a diet of boiled groundnuts, fresh coconut pieces, bananas, salads with raw greens and a little cooked rice or better still one roti or so for healthy living. She would laugh at us for roasting, frying, baking, and ultimately overeating. She said goat's milk was the best like our Mahatma, the father of the nation. Nature cure was one of her favorite topics.

'Diet is what one should worry about,' she always said. She used to read books on Siddha 'Vaidyam', Ayurveda and nature cure.

When world famous athletes and celebrities talk about the Vegan diet being the healthiest, how they feel energetic only with such a diet, the world wakes up. It is called a game changer. Our ancestors talked of Ayurveda and how good the system is for the human body. They talked about various herbs organically grown being the best for healthy living. All vitamins and minerals the human body requires are found in the vegetables and fruits was the advice given by Ayurveda. Of course yoga and Ayurveda perhaps were more preventive than curative. Indeed following these systems called for a strict and disciplined regimen and demanded some lifestyle changes too.

How I wish we were taught Yoga in school. We have started celebrating a 'yoga day' now. Yoga is hotly talked about and followed by many in the Western world and in the East too. It is gaining popularity as the world has woken up to the health benefits mankind can reap from practicing Yoga Asanas and breathing exercises like Pranayama. Similarly the researchers might recognize Ayurveda as a system of medicine for prevention of many chronic systemic problems. Our country could have included lessons on a nutritious diet with herbs and the study of herbs not only in institutions teaching Ayurveda but also as a part of the curriculum in schools and in many courses in colleges. That way the children could have learnt the virtues of living in complete harmony with nature.

What am I doing here? Going back to age old yoga and the good old herbal treatment of herbs and roots. Sorry for going back in time. When science and technology have taken mankind to the moon and on regular trips to the International Space Station. A billionaire is developing a Starship which, he says, will be a transport system, reusable too, to go to Mars!

Our scientists are trying to reach the Sun and Moon

Here she is sitting with eyes closed. Her journey is inward

35

Age is in Mind

It is said that sometime around the 90s, the then President of the USA suggested that it would be good to celebrate an international day for the older people or a day for the senior citizens or elderly or whatever. The name has been changing quite a bit. So what? 'A rose by any other name will still smell as sweet.

When I joined the senior league on the 1st of October, my friend and classmate from school reminded me that we should celebrate as we have been through it together. We chatted about school days, giggling like young girls. Actually most of us feel so young and spirited (not alcoholic) we wonder why we are looked at differently and celebrated as a separate category.

While we constantly tell ourselves that age is only a number, why does someone keep reminding us of our age? Though it is not considered good manners to ask a lady her age, especially if she is old and not a very close friend, many people, I mean, mostly, the other 60+women, do ask. I avoid answering the question with a silly joke or a sillier smile or reduce my age by 2 to 6 years depending on the person, place and the reason per se, why I am being asked. I cleverly change the topic to something more relevant or irrelevant. I keep hoping though, they never come across my 'Aadhar' card or Passport. I am not trying to say that 70 is the new 30 or 80 is the new 40 of today as these equations of sorts tend to confuse me and I might forget my actual age. The day I saw the word 'degenerated' in an 'Echocardiogram' report I knew I have stepped into the category of the old. Having lived for 80 years, I am called a super senior now. I have been through some awesome, a few awful, awkward and awe-inspiring situations.

But the fact remains that in spite of the physical degeneration, we go about our normal routine of managing the house, mumbling and grumbling though. Gone are the days when the daughters-in-law are stated to have taken over that responsibility. We have seen many such melodramatic scenes in movies of the 20th century. Sorry, I am not referring to '20th century Fox' films of Hollywood, but the Indian movies of the previous millennium.

An old mother-in-law lying on the bed would pull out a fat bunch of keys from under her pillow and hand it over to the 'bahu' with trembling hands and tears streaming down her cheeks (thanks to glycerin). Kitchen used to be the sole yet powerful domain of the women of her generation. But it is N/A to today's elderly who feel so young and outgoing, I mean feel like going out. They don't seem ready to retire as we feel age is in our mind. We want to be part of other happenings in the world outside our homes. Secondly we have no such luck in today's nuclear families. The parents and children live in different cities, countries and continents. Even if they all live in the same city, many of them prefer to live under separate roofs by mutual understanding as the lifestyle differs. In fact many things differ, starting from breakfast cereal to bedtime(TV) serial.

It is reported that the population of seniors is going up in our country, and it will supposedly go up to 175 million in a few years. It seems women will still be less than men in number. Is it the side effect of female foeticide? Whatever the statistics say or not, we know for ourselves how our lifespan has increased by at least twenty to twenty five years that is certain. Go to a wedding or to any social gathering. You see rows and rows of seniors sitting and chatting happily with people around them. They hold onto their walking sticks like mikes sometimes, as they don't want to lose their favorite ones, sticks as well as the audience around them.

You have to search desperately to see some children and youth in the crowd and start wondering what happened to the youngsters in

Youngsters in the family! It is anybody's guess; they are not locally available as they live somewhere else in the world far away from the wedding crowds. The middle aged women from the hosts' side come and greet the older lot with polite 'namaskarams'. Courteously they smile and chat for a few minutes. They request the seniors to stay for lunch, dinner etc. and then slip away slowly to the stage, where the main action takes place and videos are shot. The elderly hand over the gift pack to one of the hosts to hand it over to the bride or groom. They avoid standing in long lines and climbing steps up and down the stage when the rest of the invitees are watching. It takes time as each family starts posing for pictures with the bridal couple. But such big fat crowded weddings with a thousand guests or more mostly engage some event managers to play the role of hosts. I must say these trained youngsters manage to play the 'host' roles pretty well.

There are quite a lot of good conversationalists among the seniors who do attract the younger lot to them. They discuss every day happenings in the country. Of course the senior men will invariably go back to their hay days every other minute, especially those who had held high posts at the peak of their careers in the distant past.

In such crowded gatherings, suppose someone, whom I meet after ten years tells me, "You have not changed one bit aunty, you look the same", how happy I feel. If someone else says," Don't tell me you are seventy, aunty, you don't look a day older than 60," the day is made for me. I don't even want to think the younger women are being nice to me.

Only the previous day, a salesman, (around 50 years of age) in a cosmetics 'boutique', addressed me, "Patti, (grandma) how can I help you?" and how angry I got. What cheek, that man was not 20 years old to call me 'Patti' (grandma) and that too he did it in a boutique where I myself was feeling a bit self-conscious. I just walked out hurriedly. He moved on to attend to a pretty young girl of course.

We seniors take care to dress up well when we go out. Most of us would like to look elegant and presentable, whether we are 76 or 86. The credit goes not only to the choice of jewelry and silk sarees but also to the doctors, and the overflowing pill boxes. In fact the 7 days of a week seem to fly fast with appointments lined up for every day. The senior has an appointment with the dentist on Monday, an eye specialist on Tuesday, a podiatrist on Wednesday, maybe not for pedicure, but for painful arches, ankles, and heels. She takes appointments for Thursday in a massage parlor. Her massage may not be at a spa, but an 'Ayurveda vaidyasala'. A refreshing facial on Friday makes the old feel well groomed, rejuvenated and young by the weekend. Even bending and cutting toenails is a tough task for the aged as the nails become thick. All the calcium intake seems to make the toenails extra strong, more than the bones and teeth.

Ladies club meetings and other outings are planned days ahead. To add spice and interest some biscuits, homemade 'pakoras' or masala peanuts are packed in the picnic baskets. 'Antakshari' is a game played with great enthusiasm. The seniors attend music concerts and discourses whenever possible. Many elderly women just come wheeling in their chairs looking so confident and regal. Reality shows and contests for super singers and Indian idols on TV top the popularity lists for elderly women. I get the entire thrill watching the last 5 questions given to the woman on the hot seat in KBC, who is about to become a millionaire.

Hmm....but we tend to slow down basically in our daily activities. Naturally, how can I go fast when I keep looking down to watch every step that I take? Or turn my neck so slowly like a giraffe. Keep rolling my tongue right to left and left to right to check whether I have clots in the brain. I could be beating my fist against my palm, rubbing my hands and stretching my legs to keep them in working order. These are the outcome of WhatsApp messages of the day.

Our generation is fortunate to have medication for BP, diabetes, thyroid, arthritis, tuberculosis, and cancer too. Such diseases are diagnosed earlier as more thorough investigations are available now. The diagnostic centers look like IT offices with monitors beeping, purring, blinking and graphs being drawn. Echocardiogram shows the heart pumping 'lub-dub' to keep circulating the blood. I can watch a stent being pushed in my artery, stones in the kidneys being hit, a lump being dissolved, all on a screen in front of me. Wow. We see it all inside out. It is not scary anymore.

Waiting in the hospital lounge is not like the past. The lounges are air-conditioned, with nice seating (at times we may have to play musical chairs) and a TV screen showing ads or news or a video of one song repeatedly. Canteen is just round the corner. Toilets are available, may be slippery but reasonably clean (?) Very bad yuck, I mean luck if one falls, but at least it will be in the hospital premises. We seniors with silver crowns, gold in teeth, platinum on the necks, titanium in the joints, diamonds in our ears seem to have nerves of steel too.

The age factor is so advantageous in airports. The wheel chair brigade gets all preferences while checking in and out and in immigration queues.

To sum up I can say a few things. The house could look messy; I don't have to give an excuse. I can sleep as much as I want to. None will disturb me "Poor thing, she is too old" they may say, assuming I am fast asleep. I can binge watch TV, no time limit set for me. I can be in a nightie the whole day; none asks me to dress up properly. I am not worried if I am not trim or prim. I know if I keep laughing it will leave furrows that will make me look like the ever popular 'smiley'.

I can remain who I am if I feel young at heart.

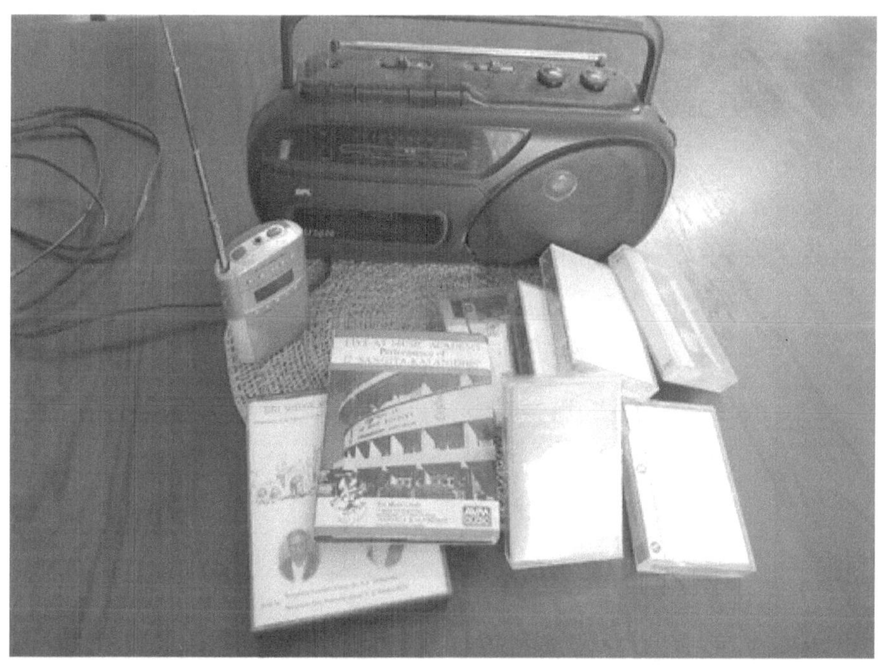

These audio and video cassettes and many other things have vanished

My Colourfull Memories

Childhood Indoor Games

Pallankuzhi (Mancala)

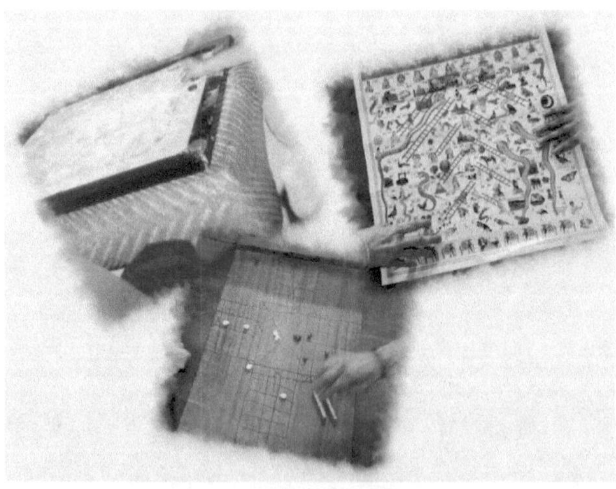

Carrom board, 'chaupar', the game of dice, Paramapada Shobhana Padam (Snakes and Ladders)

Typical sights in a village

Amma's Kitchen replicas from Bronze & Stone Age

Theyyam: Folk dance of Kerala

Festivals galore

The joy of Deepavali – crackers

A tradional Kolu with clay dolls

The festival of lamps – Karthigai Deepam

Festival of Colours – Holi

Life in Air Force

Our temporary quarters in R.K. Puram, New Delhi

Barracks at Hospital town, Jalahalli, Bangalore

Assam Tea Garden

The Huge Monitor Lizard with whom I was about to share the Bathroom

Weddings through the ages

Integrated wedding of to-day

Mehandi Celebration Prior to the Wedding

Millennial kids

Engrossed in watching TV

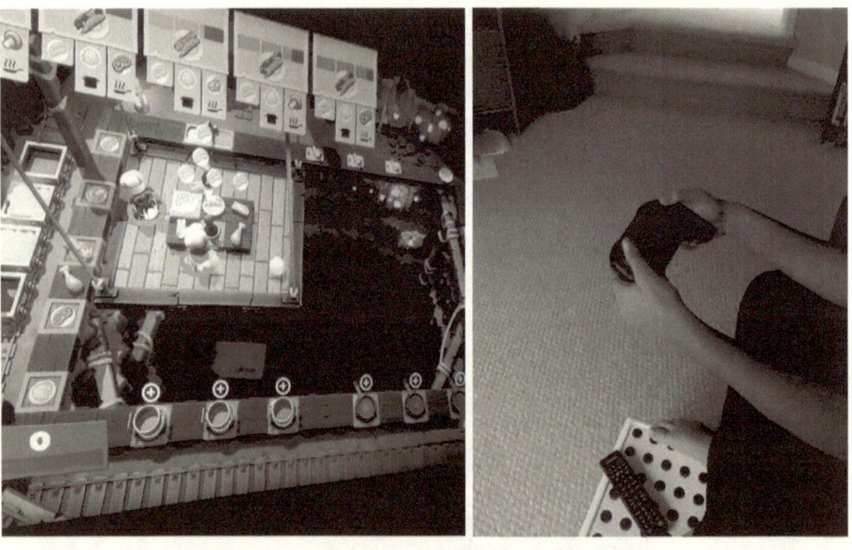

For hours on end they play on the console

Temple Chariot Festival

Shopping on the Beach!

Traffic who will take the car out first?

Most populous democracy and its success story where the spacecraft going to the Sun is there

Our scientists are trying to reach the Sun and Moon

Here she is sitting with eyes closed. Her journey is inward

www.ingramcontent.com/pod-product-compliance
Lightning Source LLC
LaVergne TN
LVHW041019150826
845672LV00001B/133

* 9 7 9 8 8 9 0 6 7 8 8 7 4 *